Mastering
APA Style

Student's Workbook and Training Guide

Sixth Edition

Mastering
APA Style

Student's Workbook and Training Guide

American Psychological Association · *Washington, DC*

Published by
American Psychological Association
750 First Street, NE
Washington, DC 20002
www.apa.org

To order
APA Order Department
P.O. Box 92984
Washington, DC 20090-2984
Tel: (800) 374-2721; Direct: (202) 336-5510
Fax: (202) 336-5502; TDD/TTY: (202) 336-6123
Online: www.apa.org/books/
E-mail: order@apa.org

In the U.K., Europe, Africa, and the Middle East, copies may be ordered from
American Psychological Association
3 Henrietta Street
Covent Garden, London
WC2E 8LU England

Typeset in Sabon, Univers, and Rockwell by Circle Graphics, Columbia, MD

Printer: Goodway Graphics, Springfield, VA
Cover Designer: Naylor Design, Washington, DC
Production Manager: Jennifer L. Macomber
Senior Editor, APA Style: Anne W. Gasque

Printed in the United States of America
Sixth Edition

Contents

Mastering

APA Style

Student's Workbook and Training Guide

The Purpose of *Mastering APA Style*

Imagine what writing would look like without style rules:
Wii the peepul uv the Youknightd Staats in oardur too form
ay moor purfekt yoonyun esstablish juctis ensur domestik
tranqilettee provid four the commen deefenc promoat the genurol
wellfair . . . oardan and establish thiss constitooshun.

What Is Style?

According to *Merriam-Webster's Collegiate Dictionary* (11th ed.),[1] *style* is "a convention with respect to spelling, punctuation, capitalization, and typographic arrangement and display followed in writing or printing" (p. 1241). When people first began to put words on paper, there were no customs or plans. Spelling was whimsical; punctuation had not been invented. There had been no need for such conventions. Listeners knew whether a speaker meant *where* or *wear* by the context of the speech. They knew when ideas were changing course because the speaker paused and drew breath. However, when people tried to read what others had written, confusion reigned. Imagine trying to read a page of text that has no commas, periods, or paragraph breaks; in which you cannot discern who is speaking because there are no quotation marks; and in which the same word may be spelled five different ways. The need for rules was immediately obvious, and style was born.

Who's on first?
Lessee hereby leases from lessor, and lessor leases to lessee, the property listed in the
attached Schedule 1 and in any schedule made a part hereof by the parties hereto
(herein called "equipment").

As soon as some uniformity had been achieved, it became obvious that exceptions to the rules, or special rules, were needed as well. Chemists needed a universally understandable, shorthand way to refer to compounds and formulas. Lawyers needed a special way of communicating that eliminated

---

[1] *Merriam-Webster's collegiate dictionary* (11th ed.). (2005). Springfield, MA: Merriam-Webster.

ambiguity in phrasing the law. Scientists needed a way of reporting the results of their experiments. Researchers needed a way of citing the sources on which their ideas were founded. Each discipline had its own needs. The style used to write a will would not be useful for writing a research article. The style used for writing a research article would not be appropriate in an office memo.

It is important to realize that there is more than one "correct" style. The style conventions that you follow for your particular writing project will be those that best meet the needs of the discipline that you are writing for or about. Thus, journalists, lawyers, government officials, literary critics, and mathematicians follow style guides that were developed specifically to meet their needs and those of their intended audiences.

What Is APA Style, and Who Uses It?

Soon after psychology was established as an academic discipline, it became clear that a customized set of rules and conventions was needed. Theories of psychology are founded on research conducted with animals and humans. The ways in which research is conducted are standardized by the discipline. For example, there are well-defined procedures for using experimental controls, applying statistics, and interpreting the validity of test scores. When preparing written reports of such research, writers must use the same conventions so that results and conclusions and the means of deriving them are universally understood.

Thus, APA Style was devised specifically to meet the needs of people who write term papers, essays, master's theses, doctoral dissertations, journal articles, reports, or books in the behavioral and social sciences. APA Style has also been widely acknowledged as a practical means to organize and communicate technical information in fields other than psychology (e.g., anthropology, sociology, nursing, management science), and many of these disciplines have adopted its use in their academic departments and professional organizations.

The handbook that lists the rules and conventions of APA Style is the *Publication Manual of the American Psychological Association*. The sixth and most current edition was published in 2010. The *Publication Manual* is widely used among writers, editors, students, and educators in the social and behavioral sciences. Hundreds of professional journals require their authors to use the *Publication Manual* as their style guide. Use of APA Style is required by all psychology departments and by many other academic departments in U.S. colleges and universities.

Why Should You Use APA Style?

The reason for using any style guide is apparent: to help you communicate your ideas clearly to others. Writing has two components: content and style. *Content* is what you say; *style* is how you say it. You may have great ideas, but if your manuscripts are not well prepared (e.g., if you make numerous grammatical errors, are repetitious, fail to cite sources, present tables that are difficult to interpret), you lose credibility with the reader. If that reader is your instructor, he or she may think that you do not understand your subject matter.

If you are a student of psychology or a related discipline, using APA Style will enable you to communicate clearly with your targeted audience. If lawyers ignored the style conventions used by their colleagues, their written work would probably be viewed with great skepticism (e.g., "When I die, give all the junk in my basement to my friend Bill, but only if he promises not to sell anything at one of his yard sales"). If statisticians invented their own way of presenting probabilities and did not use the guidelines accepted by their field, readers would have great difficulty interpreting their numbers (e.g., "The phi delta chi probability is less than gamma magna probability"). Your discipline requires you to follow APA Style—and for good reason.

What you may not realize is that you can personally benefit from using APA Style. Set aside for a moment the idea that APA Style is required, and consider what is in it for you:

- The *Publication Manual* is more than a list of rules and guidelines; it also contains sound advice on the craft of writing. Thus, APA Style will help you improve your writing skills, not only for the courses in which it is required but also for any writing that you do.
- Having rules and guidelines readily available for troublesome or complicated issues such as formatting references or displaying statistics saves you time and trouble. Because you do not have to create ways of doing these things, your time is freed up to concentrate on content.
- Often, writer's block occurs because you cannot decide how to arrange your information. Should you discuss each implication as you present each result, or should you present all of the results and then all of the implications? Should you introduce your paper by summarizing your conclusions or begin by describing your procedures and present your conclusions only at the end? There are myriad decisions to be made. The *Publication Manual* offers a ready-made outline that can help you organize your thoughts before you write and as you write.
- If you follow APA Style guidelines correctly, your writing will be free of most of the mechanical errors that can distract your readers from the ideas—the content—that you are presenting. By writing clearly, you gain the respect of your readers and their interest in your subject.
- The more you use APA Style, the more mastery you will achieve. When you achieve mastery, you will have internalized good writing skills as well as knowledge of the basic style rules. Thus, in any subsequent writing you do, you will need to consult the *Publication Manual* less and less often and will approach any writing task with greater confidence and competence. In other words, the benefits continue to accrue beyond your first term paper.
- If you plan to pursue graduate study or a professional career in psychology or a related discipline, you will probably be required to write for publication. Most publishers in your discipline require that you conform to APA Style. Thus, mastering APA Style now helps ensure your chances of success in graduate study or a professional career.
- From a purely academic standpoint, there is no question that improving your writing skills—even only the mechanics—will help you get better grades. By improving your writing, you will increase the likelihood that you will convey what you know.

Mastering APA Style has many practical advantages beyond getting you through your first course that requires it. You will save time, improve your writing skills; write with greater ease and confidence; improve your chances of getting better grades; and—most important—equip yourself with a valuable skill that will continue to serve you in the future, regardless of the career you choose.

How Will This Workbook Help You Learn APA Style?

Chances are that you are reading this book because you are required to learn APA Style. It is quite natural for you to question this requirement. You may view it as an unwelcome demand on your time. You may wonder how you can be expected to learn APA Style in addition to learning the subject matter of your course. If you do not intend to go to graduate school, you may wonder why you have to learn all of these rules just to write a few papers.

The preceding section should convince you that you will benefit from learning APA Style regardless of whether you write only one paper for a required course or go on to graduate school or a profession. Even if you are convinced that you need to learn APA Style, how will you do it? How will you find the time? Will you have to memorize the entire *Publication Manual*?

If reading a copy of the *Publication Manual* is your only means of learning APA Style, the task can seem daunting. There is much material to learn, and there are many small details to remember. Many of the guidelines may seem arbitrary to you. Thus, it may be difficult for you to understand why you should have to use them. For example, why does a paper have to be double-spaced? Why do references have to be put in alphabetical order? Why do you have to say *people with disabilities* instead of *disabled people!* As you gain experience, you will understand the practical reasons for style rules that may not be apparent at first. It is easier to learn anything if you understand its application.

You will discover that many style guidelines are intended to aid the reader. For example, double-spaced manuscripts are easier for the reviewer to read than single-spaced manuscripts, alphabetizing references makes it easier for readers to look them up, and using bias-free language shows respect and sensitivity for your audience. Some style rules, such as some of the rules for numbers, are indeed arbitrary. Such style rules exist simply because consistency is preferable.

The trouble with learning APA Style from the *Publication Manual* alone is that although examples of usage are given, the book does not offer you practice in applying rules to real-life situations. Remember that the *Publication Manual* is a reference book, not a how-to book. *Mastering APA Style* was designed to make learning APA Style easy for you and to save you time. No, you will not have to memorize the entire *Publication Manual*. In fact, memorizing the guidelines will not enable you to master APA Style. Mastery comes through practice. Think of using APA Style as a skill or a tool rather than as a subject matter to be memorized. APA Style is a means, not an end—a means of becoming your own writing critic or editor.

This user-friendly workbook is written in such a way that you may study on your own, at your own pace, without supervision. Individual instructors may offer you guidance, class time, or deadlines, all of which will also help you. The workbook also teaches through practice (i.e., hands-on learning). The exercises and tests require you to apply APA Style, not necessarily to prove that you have memorized it. Furthermore, you may not need to complete the entire workbook. The workbook is full of road markers (i.e., the sections of the *Publication Manual* to which a style point pertains are always cited), so that you can work on only those areas that you need to work on.

How to Use the *Student's Workbook and Training Guide*

Organization of the Workbook

Take a moment to look at the table of contents for the *Student's Workbook and Training Guide.* Chapter 1 described the purpose of *Mastering APA Style,* what style is in general, and what APA Style is in particular. Perhaps most important, the chapter outlined the benefits that you will gain by mastering APA Style. In this chapter, the organization and content of the workbook are described in greater detail, and instructions are given for using the materials; it is essential to read this chapter to understand how to use the materials most efficiently.

The learning materials are divided into two units: term paper writing (Chapter 3) and research report writing (Chapter 4). If you do not need to write reports of empirical research now or in the near future, you need complete only the term paper unit. However, everyone, including those who will be writing research reports, should complete the term paper unit because the basic principles it teaches are the foundation for the more technical principles taught in the research report unit. Within each unit, the learning materials are divided into four components:

- familiarization test,
- learning exercises and integrative exercises,
- practice test, and
- review exercises.

The learning, integrative, and review exercises are further subdivided by topic.

All of the answers to test and exercise items are in the workbook. The tests have answer keys, and the exercises consist of a draft version (the question) and a feedback version (the answer). You will not be left wondering whether you have correctly applied a style rule; there is no mystery. This feature of the workbook is explained more fully under "Instructions for Using the Workbook Materials" later in this chapter.

Using the *Publication Manual* With the Workbook

In the *Publication Manual,* each chapter is subdivided into numbered sections. For example, in Chapter 3, "Writing Clearly and Concisely," you will find a section coded 3.01 ("Length"). In the code 3.01, the number to the left of the decimal identifies the chapter number and the number to the right of the decimal identifies the section, which is also a specific point of style, or rule. These numbers simplify the process of finding style rules in the *Publication Manual.* The same numbering system is used in the *Student's Workbook and Training Guide* to assist you in locating the section of the *Publication Manual* pertinent to the style point you are studying. These numbers are referred to in this workbook as *APA codes,* and they are listed with each test and exercise item.

> Buy a copy of the *Publication Manual.*
>
> Always do the term paper unit first.
>
> Always take the familiarization test before doing the learning exercises.

Where Should You Begin?

Be sure you have a copy of the sixth edition of the *Publication Manual* before you begin to use the workbook. It is important to complete the term paper unit before doing the research report unit, even if you need to know APA Style only for writing research reports, because the research report unit builds on the principles taught in the term paper unit. We also recommend that you take a familiarization test before doing the learning exercises. Doing so may save you significant time and effort because it will help you identify particular style points that you have already mastered; thus, you may choose to skip the learning exercises pertaining to those points.

Although the order of the exercises corresponds roughly to the order of the sections of the *Publication Manual* indicated by APA codes, the workbook is designed for independent study and can be used flexibly. Unless your instructor makes specific assignments, you may complete the exercises in any order you find useful. To facilitate skipping around, we have included a brief synopsis preceding each topic area that lists the style points covered in the exercises and instructions for completing the exercises.

You may also wonder whether you should (a) do all of the exercises in a section (e.g., exercises on punctuation) and then go back and look at the feedback version (the correct version of each exercise item) or (b) do them one by one. Either way is fine. The same advice applies to consulting the *Publication Manual.* That is, you may consult the *Publication Manual* each time a question arises in your mind or read whole sections before or after doing the exercises. Do whatever works for you!

> Two approaches to completing learning exercises:
>
> ■ Do one exercise, jotting down changes or notes right on the workbook page. Then look at the feedback version and compare your work with the correct version. Consult the *Publication Manual* as questions arise. Go on to the next exercise.
>
> ■ Do all of the exercises in a section, jotting down changes or notes right on the workbook page. Then review all of the feedback versions. Consult the *Publication Manual* at any time.

Instructions for Using the Workbook Materials

Understanding how the materials in *Mastering APA Style* are written, arranged, and formatted before you begin working will make your task easier. The materials are described in further detail later in this chapter.

- *Mastering APA Style* consists of two books: the *Instructor's Resource Guide* and the *Student's Workbook and Training Guide*. You need only the *Student's Workbook and Training Guide*. The *Instructor's Resource Guide* contains the mastery tests, the mastery test answer keys and answer sheets, and the complete test item pool. Your instructor will provide you with any mastery test that you may be asked to take, along with an answer sheet.
- All test and exercise items cite APA codes, which indicate the sections of the *Publication Manual* that include the style guidelines pertaining to the questions and exercises.
- The tests and exercises do not cover the *Publication Manual* comprehensively. They focus on Chapters 3 through 6, which contain most of the editorial style guidelines.
- Test and exercise items are grouped by topic, and they are arranged to correspond approximately to the order of the *Publication Manual*.
- All test items are multiple-choice. There are no yes–no, true–false, or essay questions.
- The tests consist of three styles of questions: complete statements or questions, incomplete statements, and unedited segments of manuscript.
- Some of the tests and exercises are designed to help you understand and remember important aspects of APA Style, whereas others are intended to help you learn how to use the *Publication Manual* itself or to look up infrequently used technical information.

There are three styles of questions in the tests:

- complete statements or questions, for which you choose the correct response;

> 20. Which of the following examples should not be hyphenated?
>   a. role-playing technique
>   b. super-ordinate variable
>   c. six-trial problem
>   d. high-anxiety group
>   e. all of the above

- incomplete statements, for which you choose the response that accurately completes the statement (i.e., fill in the blank); and

> 21. In titles of books and articles, initial letters are capitalized in
>   a. major words when titles appear in regular text.
>   b. words of four letters or more when titles appear in regular text.
>   c. the second word in a hyphenated compound when titles appear in regular text.
>   d. major words and words of four letters or more when titles appear in reference lists.
>   e. all of the above except d.

- unedited segments of manuscripts, which you edit; you then choose the response that reflects how you edited the text.

11. Edit the following for the use of nonsexist language:

It has been suggested that the major factor giving man a performance advantage over other primates on many cognitive tasks is that the tasks have been selected and administered by other men.

a. leave as is

b. It has been suggested that the major factor giving the species of man a performance advantage over other primates on many cognitive tasks is that the tasks have been selected and administered by men of the same species.

c. It has been suggested that the major factor giving human beings a performance advantage over other primates on many cognitive tasks is that the tasks have been selected and administered by other human beings.

d. It has been suggested that the major factor giving human beings (men or women) a performance advantage over other primates on many cognitive tasks is that the tasks have been selected and administered by other human beings.

Familiarization Tests

Taking the familiarization tests and reviewing your responses to them will help you identify what you do and do not know about APA Style. The time that you spend on the familiarization tests is time well spent. In the long run, taking these tests will save you time because you will be able to focus your study efforts on only those topics that you need most to learn or master.

The tests consist of 40 numbered items, each followed by a series of possible responses identified by lowercase letters (e.g., a, b, c). Each item has only one correct response. Two answer sheets for each test are located at the end of the tests. One is blank, so that you can write in your responses. The other contains the answers and the APA codes for each item. Read each test item, read the possible responses, and write in the letter of the response that you think is correct on the blank answer sheet. You may consult the *Publication Manual* at any time. You may find it useful to make a notation next to any test item that you found to be difficult.

When you have responded to all of the test items, check your work against the answer key and score your own test. To get an accurate assessment of how much you know, count only those questions that you answered correctly without the aid of the *Publication Manual*. If the total number of incorrect answers plus looked-up answers is greater than 20% (i.e., 8 or more out of a possible 41 answers), consider doing all of the learning exercises. While you are doing the exercises, pay special attention to those aspects of APA Style that you are the least familiar with (i.e., read and practice those parts of the *Publication Manual* that you missed on the test).

However, if you did well on the familiarization test (e.g., a score of 36 or better), you may save time by skipping the learning exercises. If you are doing this work as a requirement for a course, your instructor may choose to give you a mastery test; to prepare for a mastery test, simply do the review exercises and take the practice test.

Even if you did well on the familiarization test, you may elect to go through all of the learning exercises and review exercises to strengthen your application skills. As was explained earlier, you may choose to do all of the exercises in sequence or to focus on those that deal with problem areas. For example, if the APA codes listed next to one of your incorrect responses on the test answer key are 1.03–1.05, you may want to find all of the exercises that list codes 1.03, 1.04, and 1.05 and complete those first.

Learning Exercises and Integrative Exercises

The correct version of each exercise, called the *feedback version,* always appears on the left-hand page. The incorrect version of each exercise, called the *draft version,* always appears on the right-hand page. Before beginning, we recommend that you cover up the feedback version on the left-hand page. There are two types of exercises: learning exercises and integrative exercises. *Learning exercises* are brief excerpts of text that address one or two components of APA Style. The component being targeted is shaded. Read the text and decide whether the text in the shaded area is correct or incorrect. Write corrections on the workbook page directly above the errors. By examining the feedback version of the exercise on the left-hand page, you can check the accuracy of your editing. The feedback version will state "correct as is," or the correctly edited material will be shaded. An APA code and inventory number are given for each exercise; ignore the latter.

SAMPLE LEARNING EXERCISE

Draft Version: Comma Usage

The confederate, who was going to agree with the participant, always spoke up before the confederate, who was going to disagree with the participant.

APA CODE: 4.03

Feedback Version: Comma Usage

The confederate who was going to agree with the participant always spoke up before the confederate who was going to disagree with the participant.

APA CODE: 4.03

Integrative exercises consist of a paragraph or page of text that you are instructed to edit. Style components are not targeted with shading, but you are directed to the general topic areas. Read the text carefully and edit it as you deem appropriate, writing in your changes on the draft version. On the feedback version of integrative exercises (again, always directly to your left), all essential corrections are shaded. One integrative exercise appears at the end of each topic section.

SAMPLE INTEGRATIVE EXERCISE

Draft Version: Reference Citations in Text

Research on the effects of media violence has a long tradition. Studies that address unspecific physiological arousal effects, now considered a somewhat simplistic conceptualization of emotional effects, have come under heavy criticism (Reisenzein, 1983; Cacioppo, Berntson, & Crites, 1996). Most studies also address behavioral effects of media violence, especially the effects on aggressive behavior (Murray, 2003). In contrast, emotional effects (other than effects on fear) have not been systematically addressed thus far (Wirth and Schramm, 2005).

Most research on media violence has been on fictional media, such as action movies or computer games, such as that of Bryant and Vorderer, 2006, whose primary goals are to entertain the audience and spark our emotions. According to Frijda's, 2007, "law of apparent reality," emotions are triggered primarily by events that are evaluated as real, which is why one expects that emotional effects should be stronger when one is watching nonfictional genres such as TV news. However, it has been shown that watching the news can be, in and of itself, an entertainment and social activity (McQuail, 2001). Furthermore, content analysis shows violence to be an important issue in TV news (Winterhoff-Spurk, Unz & Schwab, 2005; Winterhoff-Spurk, 1998). Thus, it seems reasonable to pay closer attention to the emotional effects of violent TV news.

APA CODES: 6.11–6.21

Feedback Version: Reference Citations in Text

Research on the effects of media violence has a long tradition. Studies that address unspecific physiological arousal effects, now considered a somewhat simplistic conceptualization of emotional effects, have come under heavy criticism (Cacioppo, Berntson, & Crites, 1996; Reisenzein, 1983). Most studies also address behavioral effects of media violence, especially the effects on aggressive behavior (Murray, 2003). In contrast, emotional effects (other than effects on fear) have not been systematically addressed thus far (Wirth & Schramm, 2005).

Most research on media violence has been on fictional media, such as action movies or computer games (e.g., Bryant & Vorderer, 2006), whose primary goals are to entertain the audience and spark our emotions. According to Frijda's (2007) "law of apparent reality," emotions are triggered primarily by events that are evaluated as real, which is why one expects that emotional effects should be stronger when one is watching nonfictional genres such as TV news. However, it has been shown that watching the news can be, in and of itself, an entertainment and social activity (McQuail, 2001). Furthermore, content analysis shows violence to be an important issue in TV news (Winterhoff-Spurk, 1998; Winterhoff-Spurk, Unz, & Schwab, 2005). Thus, it seems reasonable to pay closer attention to the emotional effects of violent TV news.

APA CODES: 6.11–6.21

Practice Tests

There are two practice tests in the workbook: one for the term paper unit and one for the research report unit. The formats of the practice and familiarization tests are the same. Answer sheets, one blank and one with answers, appear after each test. (See the earlier section on familiarization tests.) Only the purpose of the practice tests differs. They are designed to provide feedback that you can use to

- assess your level of mastery after completing the learning exercises and integrative exercises,
- decide whether to study particular topics in the *Publication Manual* in more depth,
- decide whether to go on to the review exercises, and
- decide whether to take a mastery test.

Review Exercises

All review exercises are in the integrative format. Complete these exercises in the same manner as you did the earlier integrative exercises. Review exercises are designed to give you additional practice, to help you review style points you have already studied, and to further prepare you to take a mastery test. If you had a low score on the practice test (80% or lower), you are urged to do these exercises. Similarly, if you have taken a mastery test but did not score 90% or higher, you may want to turn to these exercises before attempting another mastery test.

The exercises do not cover all of the material that is tested in the mastery tests. Some of the information in the *Publication Manual* is conceptual and cannot easily be made into concrete examples. However, we found that the conceptual material could easily be tested with multiple-choice questions.

Beyond the Workbook: Using Other Resources

The Role of Your Instructor

The role that an instructor assumes in teaching APA Style and in using this training module varies. At the beginning of the course, your instructor should describe the level of involvement he or she will have. In teaching APA Style, instructors may do the following:

- provide an overview of APA Style and use of the workbook;
- define goals and standards of achievement, that is, deadlines and criteria for demonstrating mastery;
- provide class time for instruction, questions, or taking tests;
- give feedback on performance on tests and exercises;
- administer, score, and give feedback on mastery tests; and
- supply supplemental materials such as model manuscripts that use APA Style correctly or incorrectly and tests or exercises that are different from those in your workbook. (Some of these supplemental materials are described more fully in the following sections.)

Mastery Tests

As mentioned earlier, the *Instructor's Resource Guide* contains mastery tests that you may be called on to take. Mastery tests are the primary means by which your instructor can evaluate your knowledge of APA Style and your readiness to prepare writing assignments. They are similar in structure and content to the familiarization and practice tests but contain different questions. Your instructor will score these tests; your score is often useful only for demonstrating that you have mastered APA Style (90% correct is the usual standard for mastery). There are four versions of mastery tests for each unit, so you will have more than one opportunity to demonstrate mastery. Your instructor will tell you when you will be able to take a test and how scoring will be handled in your course.

There are several differences between taking mastery tests and taking familiarization or practice tests: You will not be allowed to keep the mastery tests, you will not be given an answer key of the correct answers to keep, and you will not be permitted to use the *Publication Manual* while you take the test. Your instructor will give you feedback by checking your answer sheet, marking any incorrect responses, and giving you your score. Your instructor may give you a blank answer key (which includes the APA codes for each question) with the questions you missed marked so you can find the correct answers in the *Publication Manual*.

The *Publication Manual of the American Psychological Association*

It is essential that you have a copy of the most recent edition of the *Publication Manual*. The *Publication Manual* is the official repository of information about APA format and style, and it comprises the standards for written materials in psychology as well as many other fields. *Mastering APA Style* is designed to teach about using the *Publication Manual*, not to supplant it. The module does not cover all of the rules, standards, and guidelines that are included in the *Publication Manual*. It focuses on key elements of style and on teaching, by application, how to use the *Publication Manual* as a resource.

Other Style and Writing Guides

The *Publication Manual* is not exhaustive in its coverage of style guidelines. There are other writing and style guides to consult on matters for which the *Publication Manual* does not provide guidance.

Many institutions use *The Chicago Manual of Style*[1] as their authority. Some style guides are written for specific disciplines, such as *The Bluebook: A Uniform System of Citation*[2] for the legal profession and *Mathematics Into Type*[3] for people who need to format complicated mathematical text. These kinds of style guides may be consulted when a special need arises.

The *Publication Manual* devotes two chapters to writing style. Again, although these chapters present the fundamentals of good writing that apply to any kind of writing, they are not exhaustive and focus only on the pertinent issues faced by writers of research articles. If you discover that you need more assistance with writing, you should be aware that many good books on the topic exist. Some of these are listed at www.apastyle.org; you can also consult your reference librarian or an instructor in the English department at your school.

Model Manuscripts and Articles

One of the most effective ways to learn is through observing models. Your instructor may give you examples of written work (published and unpublished, good and bad examples). An example of an unpublished manuscript should be particularly useful for you to see. Most of the time, you will be asked to prepare manuscripts for course requirements, not publication. You may, of course, visit a library to obtain samples of manuscripts that were written according to APA Style. APA publishes numerous scholarly journals and books, and any of these would be written in APA Style. Be sure to obtain recent publications, however, to ensure that the current edition of the *Publication Manual* was followed.

Human Resources

One of the most important skills a writer can have is that of being able to edit his or her own work. Rare is the person who produces a perfect first draft; the ability to revise and to correct errors comes with experience. You may lack this experience, and it is often difficult to be objective about your own work. *Mastering APA Style* is written in a way that fosters editorial skills. You are directed to give yourself feedback (by referring to the feedback version of exercises and to relevant sections of the *Publication Manual*) and to apply that feedback to new situations.

Instructors and fellow students can provide more opportunities for giving, receiving, and applying feedback. One potentially valuable experience is to exchange your work with another student and edit each other's work. By editing another student's paper, you can gain more real-world experience as an editor, learn to be more objective about the flaws in a manuscript, and practice giving constructive criticism, all skills that will be useful to you when editing your own work.

Now You Are Ready to Begin

You have read Chapter 1 and have identified your own reasons for learning APA Style, and you understand that this training module has been written to help you do so. You have read Chapter 2 and are familiar with the contents of the workbook and how to use it. You have your own copy of the *Publication Manual*. You have set your own goals, or your instructor has set goals for you. Now you are ready to use the workbook. If at any point you are unsure of what to do next or how to use any of the materials, review the pertinent sections of Chapters 1 and 2. Of course, your instructor and your fellow students can be valuable resources.

---

[1] University of Chicago Press. (2003). *The Chicago manual of style* (15th ed.). Chicago, IL: Author.
[2] *The bluebook: A uniform system of citation* (18th ed.). (2005). Cambridge, MA: Harvard Law Review Association.
[3] Swanson, E. (1979). *Mathematics into type* (Rev. ed.). Providence, RI: American Mathematical Society.

Instructions for Taking the Term Paper Familiarization Test

Read each of the 41 numbered items and its corresponding set of possible responses, and choose the most accurate response. Each item has only one accurate response. Some of the items instruct you to edit a segment of text, which you may do right on the test, and then to choose the response that characterizes what you have done (see the examples in "Instructions for Using the Workbook Materials"). Circle your choice on the test or mark your choice on the blank answer sheet provided for you at the end of the test. Take as much time as you need to complete the test, and consult the *Publication Manual* any time you wish. You may want to mark items that give you difficulty.

After you have responded to all of the test items, check your responses against the answer key at the end of the test. Make a notation next to any incorrect response on your answer sheet. Now, look at the APA codes that are listed next to each response that is incorrect or that you have flagged as being difficult.

You may wonder why the answers are expressed in APA code intervals rather than a specific paragraph code. We found in field trials of the test materials that students attempted to learn the answer to a specific question rather than address a general weakness that they had in an area. When we gave them APA code intervals as feedback, students were less inclined to "figure out the tests" and more inclined to do what they were supposed to do: master APA Style.

These codes refer you to the relevant sections of the *Publication Manual.* You can use this feedback to gauge how much work you need to do and in what areas and to decide what course of action to take next. You may find it helpful to review particular sections of the *Publication Manual* before attempting exercises. You may proceed to the exercises and complete them all, or you may choose to do only those that pertain to style issues with which you are unfamiliar. Keeping in mind that 90% is the criterion for mastery by the time you complete the workbook, your score on the familiarization test should be your guide. If you master the familiarization test with ease (scoring 90% correct or higher), you may even decide to do only the review exercises or go on to the practice test.

SAMPLE "EDIT THE FOLLOWING" QUESTION

19. Edit the following for the punctuation of a series:

   Theories of work motivation that emphasize the cognitive effects of information include a expectancy theory, b equity theory, and c goal-setting theory.

   a. leave as is
   b. Theories of work motivation that emphasize the cognitive effects of information include (a) expectancy theory, (b) equity theory, and (c) goal-setting theory.
   c. Theories of work motivation that emphasize the cognitive effects of information include a) expectancy theory, b) equity theory, and c) goal-setting theory.
   d. Theories of work motivation that emphasize the cognitive effects of information include: a. expectancy theory, b. equity theory, and c. goal-setting theory.

Instructions for Completing the Exercises

In the sample learning exercise that follows, each exercise consists of two elements: the text of the exercise and the APA code. The APA code cites the section of the *Publication Manual* that the exercise addresses. Approach the exercises as follows: Do not look at the feedback version on the left-hand page until you have completed working with the draft version on the right-hand page. Read the text in the draft version (right-hand page). Examine the text that is shaded and decide whether it is correct as is or needs to be edited. Write changes on or above the text lines. If you consult the *Publication Manual*, refer to the APA codes to find the pertinent sections. You may complete all of the exercises and then look at the feedback version, or you may look at the feedback version after completing each exercise.

Read the feedback version of each exercise (left-hand page) and examine the text that is shaded. Compare your editing with the correct version. If your response does not agree with the feedback version, you may want to review relevant sections of the *Publication Manual*.

SAMPLE LEARNING EXERCISE

Draft Version: That Versus Which

The training technique which was easiest to administer turned out to be the one that was most effective.

APA CODE: 3.22

Feedback Version: That Versus Which

The training technique that was easiest to administer turned out to be the one that was most effective.

APA CODE: 3.22

For integrative exercises (see the example following), read the text of the draft version and edit as needed by writing changes on or above the text lines. None of the text is shaded; you must decide which style points are being addressed. Consult the *Publication Manual* by referring to the APA codes listed with the exercise. When you have finished editing the draft version, consult the feedback version. With integrative exercises, it is probably best if you do this after each exercise, while your reasoning is still fresh in your mind. Essential changes will be shaded on the feedback version, or the exercise will indicate that the text is "correct as is."

SAMPLE INTEGRATIVE EXERCISE

Draft Version: Headings and Series

Irrational Fear

Fear of salamanders

Forest newt phobia. There is a salamander found near Salamanca, New York, a tiny pink and white forest newt, that has been shown to arouse tremendous fear in people who already have (a) a spaghetti phobia, (b) a worm phobia, and (c) mysophobia.

APA CODES: 3.03–3.04

Feedback Version: Headings and Series

IRRATIONAL FEAR

Fear of Salamanders

Forest newt phobia. There is a salamander found near Salamanca, New York, a tiny pink and white forest newt, that has been shown to arouse tremendous fear in people who already have (a) a spaghetti phobia, (b) a worm phobia, and (c) mysophobia.

APA CODES: 3.03–3.04

Term Paper Unit

3

The purpose of this unit is to familiarize you with the basic principles of APA Style, such as grammar, spelling, and hyphenation, as they apply to writing term papers, essays, and literature reviews. This unit is divided into four components: the familiarization test, learning exercises and integrative exercises, the practice test, and review exercises. Begin by taking the familiarization test, which will help you to identify what you do and do not know about APA Style.

Term Paper Familiarization Test

Taking this 41-question multiple-choice test will help you determine the style principles with which you need more practice. There are two answer sheets at the end of the test, one with blanks for you to write in your answers and the other containing the correct answers.

Beside each blank you will find the APA code (e.g., 1.03, 2.13) that indicates where you can find the answer to that question in the *Publication Manual*. These APA codes correspond to the numbered sections of the *Publication Manual*. Read each test item and the possible responses, and write the letter of the response on the blank answer sheet. You may consult the *Publication Manual* at any time. It may be useful to mark questions you found to be difficult.

After taking this test, check your answers against the answer key and score your test, but count only those questions that you answered without using the *Publication Manual*. If the total number of incorrect answers plus looked-up answers is 8 or more (20% or more incorrect), we advise you to complete all of the exercises that follow this test. If you did well on the test (i.e., 36 of 41 correct), you may want to skip the learning exercises and take the practice test that follows the exercises in this term paper unit or take a mastery test.

TERM PAPER FAMILIARIZATION TEST

1. In contrast to empirical studies or theoretical articles, literature reviews

    a. define and clarify a problem.

    b. summarize previous investigations.

    c. identify relations, contradictions, or inconsistencies in the literature.

    d. suggest steps for future research.

    e. do all of the above.

2. When listing an author of a paper, it is incorrect to

    a. give titles (PhD or OFM).

    b. spell out the middle name.

    c. use informal names (Marty Seligman).

    d. do all of the above.

3. The headings of a manuscript should

    a. reveal the logical organization of the paper to the reader.

    b. be at the same level for topics of equal importance.

    c. not be labeled with numbers or letters.

    d. do all of the above.

4. Which example is correct for an article in which four levels of heading are required?

    a.

A History of Psychology

Early Laboratories

    Harvard laboratories.

    James's basement.

    b.

A History of Psychology

Early Laboratories

Harvard Laboratories

    James's basement.

    c.

A HISTORY OF PSYCHOLOGY

    Early Laboratories

Harvard Laboratories

James's basement.

    d.

A HISTORY OF PSYCHOLOGY

Early Laboratories

    Harvard laboratories.

    James's basement.

5. Edit the following for the presentation of a series:

The researchers attempted to determine the relation between the age of the mother at the child's birth and (1) the child's intellectual development, (2) the child's social development, and (3) the mother's personal adjustment.

   a. leave as is
   b. The researchers attempted to determine the relation between the age of the mother at the child's birth and (a) the child's intellectual development, (b) the child's social development, and (c) the mother's personal adjustment.
   c. The researchers attempted to determine the relation between the age of the mother at the child's birth and a) the child's intellectual development, b) the child's social development, and c) the mother's personal adjustment.
   d. The researchers attempted to determine the relation between the age of the mother at the child's birth and (A) the child's intellectual development, (B) the child's social development, and (C) the mother's personal adjustment.

6. In casual conversation the word *since* is synonymous with _____, but in scientific writing it should be used only in its temporal meaning.

   a. *however*
   b. *because*
   c. *after*
   d. all of the above

7. Good economy of expression may be achieved through using

   a. short words.
   b. short sentences.
   c. direct, simple declarative sentences.
   d. short paragraphs.
   e. all of the above.

8. The phrase "the experiment demonstrated" is an example of which of the following writing errors?

   a. ambiguity
   b. redundancy
   c. anthropomorphism
   d. none of the above

9. Edit the following for avoiding gender bias:

It has been suggested that the major factor giving man a performance advantage over other primates on many cognitive tasks is that the tasks have been selected and administered by other men.

   a. leave as is
   b. It has been suggested that the major factor giving the species of man a performance advantage over other primates on many cognitive tasks is that the tasks have been selected and administered by men of the same species.
   c. It has been suggested that the major factor giving human beings a performance advantage over other primates on many cognitive tasks is that the tasks have been selected and administered by other human beings.
   d. It has been suggested that the major factor giving human beings (men or women) a performance advantage over other primates on many cognitive tasks is that the tasks have been selected and administered by other human beings.

10. Edit the following for avoiding bias in racial and ethnic identity:

Because of their cultural deprivation, children in Third World countries have fewer opportunities to develop our moral values.

   a. leave as is
   b. Because of cultural differences, children in Third World countries may develop moral values different from those of children in Western countries.
   c. Because of their cultural deprivation, children in Third World countries may not develop higher moral values.
   d. Because of their cultural experiences, children in Third World countries have fewer opportunities to develop our moral values.

11. Which of the following sentences contains the preferable use of verb tense and voice?

   a. The same results have been shown by Komarraju (2008).
   b. Komarraju (2008) shows the same results.
   c. Komarraju (2008) showed the same results.
   d. Komarraju (2008) had shown the same results.

12. Which of the following sentences is an example of correct agreement between the pronoun and its antecedent?

   a. The instructions that were included in the experiment were complex.
   b. Neither the highest scorer nor the lowest scorer had any doubt about their competence.
   c. The group improved their scores 30%.
   d. All of the above are correct.
   e. None of the above is correct.

13. Edit the following for the placement of the modifier *only:*

Although the authors reported the data for the mild and extreme patients in the placebo condition, they only reported the data for the extreme patients in the treatment condition.

   a. leave as is
   b. Although the authors reported the data for the mild and extreme patients in the placebo condition, they reported only the data for the extreme patients in the treatment condition.
   c. Although the authors reported the data for the mild and extreme patients in the placebo condition, they reported the data for only the extreme patients in the treatment condition.
   d. Although the authors reported the data for the mild and extreme patients in the placebo condition, they reported the data for the extreme patients only in the treatment condition.

14. Edit the following for the use of subordinate conjunctions:

Since left-handers constitute a minority of the population, there are less likely to be appropriate models for them to watch.

   a. leave as is
   b. Because left-handers constitute a minority of the population, there are less likely to be appropriate models for them to watch.
   c. Although left-handers constitute a minority of the population, there are less likely to be appropriate models for them to watch.
   d. While left-handers constitute a minority of the population, there are less likely to be appropriate models for them to watch.

15. Edit the following for sentence structure:

Erikson's psychosocial theory emphasizes not only developmental stages but also the role of the ego.

   a. leave as is
   b. Erikson's psychosocial theory not only emphasizes developmental stages but also the role of the ego.
   c. Erikson's psychosocial theory emphasizes not only developmental stages but also the role of the ego, as well.
   d. Erikson's psychosocial theory emphasizes not only developmental stages but neither the role of the ego.

16. One space should follow

   a. semicolons.
   b. colons in two-part titles.
   c. periods in the initials of personal names.
   d. all of the above.
   e. none of the above.

17. Edit the following for punctuation:

    The James–Lange theory of emotion states that our emotional experience is caused by our awareness of our bodily reaction to some stimulus: Schachter and Singer (1962) proposed that a cognitive evaluation mediates between the bodily reaction and the subjective emotion.

    a. leave as is
    b. The James–Lange theory of emotion states that our emotional experience is caused by our awareness of our bodily reaction to some stimulus. Schachter and Singer (1962) proposed that a cognitive evaluation mediates between the bodily reaction and the subjective emotion.
    c. The James–Lange theory of emotion states that our emotional experience is caused by our awareness of our bodily reaction to some stimulus—Schachter and Singer (1962) proposed that a cognitive evaluation mediates between the bodily reaction and the subjective emotion.
    d. The James–Lange theory of emotion states that our emotional experience is caused by our awareness of our bodily reaction to some stimulus. And Schachter and Singer (1962) proposed that a cognitive evaluation mediates between the bodily reaction and the subjective emotion.

18. Which of the following phrases is correctly punctuated?

    a. the study, by Wenzel Brown and Beck (2008)
    b. the study by Wenzel, Brown, and Beck (2008)
    c. the study by Wenzel, Brown, and Beck, (2008)
    d. the study by Wenzel, Brown and Beck (2008)
    e. the study by Wenzel Brown and Beck (2008)

19. Edit the following for the punctuation of a reference entry:

    VandenBos, G. R. (Ed). (2007). *APA dictionary of psychology*. Washington, DC, American Psychological Association.

    a. leave as is
    b. VandenBos, G. R. (Ed.). (2007). *APA dictionary of psychology*. Washington, DC: American Psychological Association.
    c. VandenBos, G.R. (Ed.) (2007). *APA dictionary of psychology*. Washington: American Psychological Association.
    d. VandenBos, G.R.(Ed.). (2007). *APA dictionary of psychology*. Washington DC: American Psychological Association.

20. When is the em dash used?

    a. to extend a thought
    b. instead of commas to set off restrictive clauses
    c. never in APA articles
    d. to indicate a sudden interruption in the continuity of a sentence

21. Edit the following for the correct way to report verbatim instructions:

    The participants were instructed to COMPLETE EACH SENTENCE BASED ON YOUR OWN FEELINGS AT THIS MOMENT.

    a. leave as is
    b. The participants were instructed to *complete each sentence based on your own feelings at this moment.*
    c. The participants were instructed to "complete each sentence based on your own feelings at this moment."
    d. The participants were instructed to 'complete each sentence based on your own feelings at this moment.'

22. When quoting long sections of material (e.g., verbatim instructions to participants of more than 40 words),

    a. set the quote off with double quotation marks.
    b. indent and use a block format without any quotation marks.
    c. use a single quotation at the beginning and the end of the quotation.
    d. use double quotation marks and single-spacing.

23. Edit the following for the punctuation of a series:

    Theories of work motivation that emphasize the cognitive effects of information include *a* expectancy theory, *b* equity theory, and *c* goal-setting theory.

    a. leave as is
    b. Theories of work motivation that emphasize the cognitive effects of information include (a) expectancy theory, (b) equity theory, and (c) goal-setting theory.
    c. Theories of work motivation that emphasize the cognitive effects of information include a) expectancy theory, b) equity theory, and c) goal-setting theory.
    d. Theories of work motivation that emphasize the cognitive effects of information include: a. expectancy theory, b. equity theory, and c. goal-setting theory.

24. Which of the following examples should not be hyphenated?

    a. role-playing technique
    b. super-ordinate variable
    c. six-trial problem
    d. high-anxiety group
    e. all of the above

25. In titles of books and articles, initial letters are capitalized in

    a. major words when titles appear in regular text.
    b. words of four letters or more when titles appear in regular text.
    c. the second word in a hyphenated compound when titles appear in regular text.
    d. major words and words of four letters or more when titles appear in reference lists.
    e. all of the above except d.

26. From the following choices, select the sentence with the correct use of italics:

    a. She published her results in the *Journal of Interpersonal Relations and Social Behavior.*

    b. She published *her* results in the Journal of Interpersonal Relations and Social Behavior.

    c. When the *participants* read the nonsense syllable gux, they had to soothe their fearful partners.

    d. *Albino rabbits,* oryctolagus cuniculus, were given unconditional positive regard in both experimental groups.

27. Edit the following for use of abbreviations:

    According to Pavlov (1927), the conditioned stimulus (CS) should be delivered about 1 s before the unconditioned stimulus (US).

    a. leave as is

    b. According to Pavlov (1927), the conditioned stimulus (CS) should be delivered about 1 second before the unconditioned stimulus (US).

    c. According to Pavlov (1927), the conditioned stimulus (CS) should be delivered about 1 sec. before the unconditioned stimulus (US).

    d. According to Pavlov (1927), the CS should be delivered about 1 s before the US.

28. Identify the error in the following quotation:

    The author speculated that "negative exemplars within the self-concept are more confidently known than affirmative exemplars" (Brinthaup, 1983).

    a. The quotation is correctly cited.

    b. The quotation should be in block form.

    c. Quotation marks are not necessary.

    d. A page number should be cited.

29. Edit the following for the citation of a reference in text:

    Among epidemiological samples, Kessler (p. 67) found that early onset social anxiety disorder results in a more potent and severe course.

    a. leave as is

    b. Among epidemiological samples, Kessler (Kessler, 2003), found that early onset social anxiety disorder results in a more potent and severe course.

    c. Among epidemiological samples, Kessler found that early onset social anxiety disorder results in a more potent and severe course

    d. Among epidemiological samples, Kessler (2003) found that early onset social anxiety disorder results in a more potent and severe course.

30. Edit the following for the citation of a reference in text:

    A low Factor of informant consensus (F_{ic}) value indicates that the informants disagree on the taxa to be used in the treatment within a category of illness (Schlage, Mabula, Mahunnah, & Heinrich, 2000; Owuor & Kisangau, 2006). Schlage and others (2000) used F_{ic} to evaluate the ethnobotanical importance of the medicinal plants of Washambaa in Tanzania.

    a. leave as is
    b. A low Factor of informant consensus (F_{ic}) value indicates that the informants disagree on the taxa to be used in the treatment within a category of illness (Schlage, Mabula, Mahunnah, Heinrich, 2000; Owuor & Kisangau, 2006). Schlage used F_{ic} to evaluate the ethnobotanical importance of the medicinal plants of Washambaa in Tanzania.
    c. A low Factor of informant consensus (F_{ic}) value indicates that the informants disagree on the taxa to be used in the treatment within a category of illness (Owuor & Kisangau, 2006; Schlage, Mabula, Mahunnah, Heinrich, 2000). Schlage, Mabula, Mahunnah, and Heinrich used F_{ic} to evaluate the ethnobotanical importance of the medicinal plants of Washambaa in Tanzania.
    d. A low Factor of informant consensus (F_{ic}) value indicates that the informants disagree on the taxa to be used in the treatment within a category of illness (Owuor & Kisangau, 2006; Schlage, Mabula, Mahunnah, & Heinrich, 2000). Schlage et al. (2000) used F_{ic} to evaluate the ethnobotanical importance of the medicinal plants of Washambaa in Tanzania.

31. When a publication has no author,

    a. the text citation should list the author as Anonymous.
    b. the text citation should use the publisher's name.
    c. no citation is necessary.
    d. none of the above is true.

32. Edit the following for the citation of references in text:

    Several parameters for rehabilitation psychology research need to be established to improve evidence-based intervention and therapy in this field (Tate, Findley, Dijkers, Nobunaga, & Karunas, 1999; Tate, 2001; Tate, 2006). Personality changes may also occur later in life (Neugarten, 1973; Neugarten & Hagestad, 1976; Neugarten, 1977).

    a. leave as is
    b. Several parameters for rehabilitation psychology research need to be established to improve evidence-based intervention and therapy in this field (Tate, 2001, 2006; Tate, Findley, Dijkers, Nobunaga, & Karunas, 1999). Personality changes may also occur later in life (Neugarten, 1973, 1977; Neugarten & Hagestad, 1976).
    c. Several parameters for rehabilitation psychology research need to be established to improve evidence-based intervention and therapy in this field (Tate, 2001; Tate, 2006; Tate, Findley, Dijkers, Nobunaga, & Karunas, 1999). Personality changes may also occur later in life (Neugarten, 1973, 1977; & Hagestad, 1976).
    d. Several parameters for rehabilitation psychology research need to be established to improve evidence-based intervention and therapy in this field (Tate, 2001, 2006; & Findley, Dijkers, Nobunaga, & Karunas, 1999). Personality changes may also occur later in life (Neugarten, 1973, Neugarten & Hagestad, 1976; ibid., 1977).

33. When citing a specific part of a source, be sure to give

    a. the authors' names.
    b. the year of publication.
    c. a page number, paragraph number, or nearby heading and paragraph number if a quotation is cited.
    d. all of the above.

34. Who has the responsibility to ensure that references are accurate and complete?

    a. an editor
    b. a proofreader
    c. peer reviewer
    d. an author

35. Edit the following for ordering the references in a reference list. Choose the sequence of numbers that indicates the correct order of the four references. (*Note:* The numbers are not part of APA Style but are used here for brevity.)

    1. Ben-Zeev, T., & Star, J. (2001). Intuitive mathematics: Theoretical and educational implications. In B. Torff & R. Sternberg (Eds.), *The Educational Psychology Series. Understanding and teaching the intuitive mind: Student and teacher learning* (pp. 29–56). Mahwah, NJ: Erlbaum.

    2. Ben-Zeev, T., Duncan, S., & Forbes, C. (2005). Stereotypes and math performance. In J. I. D. Campbell (Ed.), *Handbook of mathematical cognition* (pp. 235–249). New York, NY: Psychology Press.

    3. Bender, W. N., Vail, C. O., & Scott, K. (1995). Teachers' attitudes toward increased mainstreaming: Implementing effective instruction for students with learning disabilities. *Journal of Learning Disabilities, 28,* 87–84, 120. doi:10.1177/002221949502800203

    4. Bender, W. N. (2005). *Differentiating math instruction: Strategies that work for K–8 classrooms!* Thousand Oaks, CA: Corwin Press.

    a. leave as is (i.e., 1, 2, 3, 4)
    b. 3, 4, 1, 2
    c. 3, 1, 4, 2
    d. 4, 3, 2, 1

36. Edit the following for the application of APA reference style:

Lassen, S. R., Steele, M. M., & Sailor, W. The relationship of school-wide positive behavior support to academic achievement in an urban middle school. *Psychology in the Schools, 43,* 701–712. (2006). doi:10.1002/pits.20177

a. leave as is

b. Lassen, S. R., Steele, M. M., & Sailor, W. 2006. The relationship of school-wide positive behavior support to academic achievement in an urban middle school. *Psychology in the Schools, 43,* 701–712. doi:10.1002/pits.20177

c. Lassen, S. R., Steele, M. M., & Sailor, W. (2006) The relationship of school-wide positive behavior support to academic achievement in an urban middle school. *Psychology in the Schools, 43,* 701–712. doi:10.1002/pits.20177

d. Lassen, S. R., Steele, M. M., & Sailor, W. (2006). The relationship of school-wide positive behavior support to academic achievement in an urban middle school. *Psychology in the Schools, 43,* 701–712. doi:10.1002/pits.20177

37. Edit the following for the application of APA reference style:

Real Academia Española. (2001). *Diccionario de la lengua española, 22nd ed.* [Dictionary of the Spanish language]. Madrid: Author.

a. leave as is

b. Real Academia Española. (2001). *Diccionario de la lengua española* [Dictionary of the Spanish language, 22nd ed.]. Madrid, Spain: Author.

c. Real Academia Española. (2001). *Diccionario de la lengua española* [Dictionary of the Spanish language] (22nd ed.). Madrid, Spain: Author.

d. Real Academia Española. (2001). *Diccionario de la lengua española* [Dictionary of the Spanish language: Twenty-second edition]. Madrid, Spain: Author.

38. What is the digital object identifier or DOI?

a. a unique alphanumeric string assigned by a registration agency (the International DOI Foundation).

b. a unique identifier that should only be used if the URL is too long.

c. a unique identifier that identifies content and provides a persistent link to its location on the Internet.

d. both a and c.

e. none of the above.

39. When typing a paper,

a. double-space after headings and between paragraphs and reference list citations; single-space elsewhere.

b. double-space throughout the paper; single- or one-and-a-half spacing may be used in tables or figures.

c. single-space between the lines of table headings.

d. double-space everything except triple-space after major headings.

40. Edit the following by selecting the correct spacing and margin arrangement for the first sentence of a paragraph:

    The mating and social behaviors of many species change dramatically when they are removed from their natural environments, whether to be domesticated or to be exhibited in zoos.

    a. leave as is

    b.   The mating and social behaviors of many species change dramatically when they are removed from their natural environments, whether to be domesticated or to be exhibited in zoos.

    c.   The mating and social behaviors of many species change dramatically when they are removed from their natural environments, whether to be domesticated or to be exhibited in zoos.

41. Changes to proofs should not include

    a. corrections of production errors.
    b. updates to reference citations.
    c. rewritten text the author would like to insert.
    d. corrections to changes in meaning in text.

TERM PAPER FAMILIARIZATION TEST
ANSWER SHEET AND FEEDBACK REPORT

Student Name _____ **Date** _____

Question Number	Answer	APA Codes	Question Number	Answer	APA Codes
1	_____	1.01–1.06	22	_____	4.01–4.11
2	_____	2.02–2.03	23	_____	4.01–4.11
3	_____	3.02–3.03	24	_____	4.12–4.13
4	_____	3.02–3.03	25	_____	4.14–4.20
5	_____	3.04	26	_____	4.21
6	_____	3.05, 3.22	27	_____	4.22–4.30
7	_____	3.08	28	_____	6.01–6.08
8	_____	3.09	29	_____	6.11–6.19
9	_____	3.12–3.17	30	_____	6.11–6.19
10	_____	3.12–3.17	31	_____	6.11–6.19
11	_____	3.18–3.19	32	_____	6.11–6.19
12	_____	3.20–3.23	33	_____	6.11–6.19
13	_____	3.20–3.23	34	_____	6.22–6.25
14	_____	3.20–3.23	35	_____	6.22–6.25
15	_____	3.20–3.23	36	_____	6.22–6.25
16	_____	4.01–4.11	37	_____	6.27–6.31
17	_____	4.01–4.11	38	_____	6.31
18	_____	4.01–4.11	39	_____	8.03
19	_____	4.01–4.11	40	_____	8.03
20	_____	4.01–4.11	41	_____	8.06
21	_____	4.01–4.11			

NUMBER CORRECT _____

TERM PAPER FAMILIARIZATION TEST
ANSWER KEY

Question Number	Answer	APA Codes	Question Number	Answer	APA Codes
1	e	1.01–1.06	22	b	4.01–4.11
2	d	2.02–2.03	23	b	4.01–4.11
3	d	3.02–3.03	24	b	4.12–4.13
4	a	3.02–3.03	25	e	4.14–4.20
5	b	3.04	26	a	4.21
6	b	3.05, 3.22	27	a	4.22–4.30
7	e	3.08	28	d	6.01–6.08
8	c	3.09	29	d	6.11–6.19
9	c	3.12–3.17	30	d	6.11–6.19
10	b	3.12–3.17	31	d	6.11–6.19
11	c	3.18–3.19	32	b	6.11–6.19
12	a	3.20–3.23	33	d	6.11–6.19
13	c	3.20–3.23	34	d	6.22–6.25
14	b	3.20–3.23	35	d	6.22–6.25
15	a	3.20–3.23	36	d	6.22–6.25
16	d	4.01–4.11	37	c	6.27–6.31
17	b	4.01–4.11	38	d	6.31
18	b	4.01–4.11	39	b	8.03
19	b	4.01–4.11	40	b	8.03
20	d	4.01–4.11	41	c	8.06
21	c	4.01–4.11			

Term Paper Learning Exercises and Integrative Exercises

There are two types of exercises in this section: learning (short) exercises and integrative exercises. Learning exercises are brief excerpts of text that address one or two components of APA Style (e.g., commas, capitalization). Integrative exercises consist of a paragraph or page of text that you need to edit. The learning exercises and integrative exercises appear in two versions: *draft,* which may or may not contain errors, and *feedback,* which shows the corrections. The feedback (correct) version always appears on the left-hand page and the draft (incorrect) version on the right. There are APA codes under each section title that indicate where the specific style rules can be found in the *Publication Manual;* APA codes corresponding to the sections of the *Publication Manual* are also below each exercise. In the learning exercises, the component that is being targeted (i.e., in need of correction) is shaded. Looking at the draft version on the right-hand page, read the text and decide whether the shaded text is correct or incorrect. Write corrections on the workbook page directly above the errors. Consult the *Publication Manual* at any time. Check your answers against the feedback version of the same exercise on the left to see whether you edited the exercise correctly. The feedback version will state "correct as is," or the correctly edited material will be shaded. You may complete the exercises and check the corrections one by one or section by section.

In the integrative exercises, the components in need of correction are not shaded, but the errors in each exercise are related to the style rules applied in the preceding learning exercises. For example, if you are working in the section on italics, the errors you will be looking for involve the use of italics. Read the text carefully and edit it as you deem appropriate, marking corrections directly on the draft version. The corrections are shaded on the feedback (left-hand) page. Integrative exercises follow the learning exercises. After completing the exercises, you can take the term paper practice test that follows the exercises, or you can ask your instructor to give you a mastery test.

Parts of a Manuscript
APA Codes: 2.01–2.13, 8.03

NOTES:

Effects of Long-Term Memory on Artificial Intelligence

Ebbin G. Haus

Mnemonia University

APA CODE: 2.01

Can I Give You a Hand, a Hand, . . . a Hand? Hyperaltruism in
the Octopus

Minnie Foote and Hans Goode

Submarine Social Center, Atlantis University

APA CODE: 2.02

Running head: BOVINE BARNYARD BANTER

Naturalistic Observation of Barnyard Banter: Pig

Latin Epithets Overheard During Bovine Horseplay

Hans Clever and Du Li Tal

Interspecies Babble Institute, Babylonia, Babylon

APA CODE: 8.03

Parts of a Manuscript
APA Codes: 2.01–2.13, 8.03

These exercises cover typing the title page, author affiliation, and running heads (see the *Publication Manual* sections 2.01–2.13 and 8.03). Mark corrections directly on the right-hand page, and compare your responses with the correct answers on the left-hand page. When you are finished with this section, go on to the next section on which you need practice.

A Study of the Effects of LTM on AI

Ebbin G. Haus

Mnemonic: University

APA CODE: 2.01

Can I Give You a Hand, a Hand, . . . a Hand? Hyperaltruism in
the Octopus

Foote, Minnie   Goode, Hans

Submarine Social Center, Atlantis University

APA CODE: 2.02

Running head: BOVINE BARNYARD BANTER

Naturalistic Observation of Barnyard Banter:
Pig-Latin Epithets Overheard During Bovine Horseplay

Hans Clever and Du Li Tal

Interspecies Babble Institute, Babylon, Babylonia

APA CODE: 8.03

Running head: COMPARATIVE HOSTILITY IN RATTLESNAKES

Latent Hostility in Tongue-in-Cheek Expressions: Phylogenetic Comparison of
Rattlesnakes (*Crotolus bitus*) and Humans (*Homo sapiens*)

Rip Tyle

Desert Rock State College

V. Shus and Hugh Moor

School of Hard Knocks College

Correct as is.

APA CODE: 2.02

Running head: PSYCHOPHYSIOLOGY OF STRESSED CUCUMBERS

Cool as a Cucumber: Psychophysiological Responses of a Vegetative

Organism to Social and Emotional Stressors

Bess T. Green, Vera Thigsken, and Sal Ad O'yil

Seedy Character College

APA CODE: 2.02

Running head: COMPARATIVE HOSTILITY IN RATTLESNAKES

Latent Hostility in Tongue-in-Cheek Expressions: Phylogenetic Comparison of
Rattlesnakes (*Crotolus bitus*) and Humans (*Homo sapiens*)

Rip Tyle

Desert Rock State College

V. Shus and Hugh Moor

School of Hard Knocks College

APA CODE: 2.02

Running head: PSYCHOPHYSIOLOGY OF STRESSED CUCUMBERS

COOL AS A CUCUMBER: PSYCHOPHYSIOLOGICAL RESPONSES OF A VEGETATIVE ORGANISM TO

SOCIAL AND EMOTIONAL STRESSORS

Bess T. Green, Vera Thigsken, and Sal Ad O'yil

Seedy Character College

APA CODE: 2.02

Running head: VICIOUS CIRCLE BEHAVIOR

3

Vicious Circle Behavior and Parental Child Abuse

APA CODES: 2.02, 8.03

Running head: VALIDITY OF DRONE INTERVIEWS

Meta-Analysis of Predictive Validity of the Personal Interview for Selecting Apiary Workers:

A Stinging Critique

Queen Bea H. Ivy

Wasp Personnel Consultants, Buzztown, New Colony

APA CODE: 8.03

Integrative Exercise: Parts of a Manuscript

Running head: SEVERE WEATHER AND OLFACT1ON

1

A Study of Effects of Severe Weather Conditions on Olfactory Sensitivity

O. Dora Testor, Cy Clone, Harry Cane, and Thor Naddo

University of the North

APA CODES: 2.01–2.02, 8.03

Vicious Circle Behavior and Parental Child Abuse

APA CODES: 2.02, 8.03

Running head: VALIDITY OF DRONE INTERVIEWS

Meta-Analysis of Predictive Validity of the Personal Interview for

Selecting Apiary Workers: A Stinging Critique

Queen Bea H. Ivy

Wasp Personnel Consultants, Buzztown, New Colony

APA CODE: 8.03

Integrative Exercise: Parts of a Manuscript

1

A STUDY OF EFFECTS OF SEVERE WEATHER CONDITIONS ON OLFACTORY

SENSITIVITY

O. Dora Testor   Cy Clone, Harry Cane and Thor Naddo

Department of Psychology   Department of Psychometeorology

University of the North

Running head: SEVERE WEATHER AND OLFACTION

APA CODES: 2.01–2.02, 8.03

Headings and Series
APA Codes: 3.02–3.04

NOTES:

The Social Psychology of Rumors

Wish Rumors

Dread Rumors

    Disease rumors.

    Disaster rumors.

    Invasion rumors.

Conclusion

References

APA CODES: 3.02–3.03

The Social Psychology of Rumors

Disaster Rumors

Conflict Rumors

Wish Rumors

Emotions and Rumor Transmission

References

APA CODE: 3.03

Headings and Series
APA Codes: 3.02–3.04

This group of exercises will help you learn to organize a manuscript with headings, to select the levels of headings, and to clearly present series (see the *Publication Manual*, sections 3.02–3.04). Mark corrections directly on the right-hand page, and compare your responses with the correct answers on the left-hand page. When you are finished with this section, go on to the next section on which you need practice.

The Social Psychology of Rumors

Wish Rumors

Dread Rumors

    Disease rumors.

    Disaster rumors.

    Invasion rumors.

Conclusion

References

APA CODES: 3.02–3.03

Introduction

The Social Psychology of Rumors

Disaster Rumors

Conflict Rumors

Wish Rumors

Emotions and Rumor Transmission

References

APA CODE: 3.03

Social Skills Training

Preliminary Measures

Sociability.

APA CODE: 3.03

The adolescents were divided into 18 groups according to whether they selected a role model who was (a) Black, White, or Cuban; (b) male or female; and (c) an athlete, entertainer, or scientist.

APA CODE: 3.04

Integrative Exercise: Headings and Series

Irrational Fear

Fear of Living Organisms

Amphibian phobias.

Fear of salamanders.

Forest newt phobia. There is a salamander found near Salamanca, New York, a tiny pink and white forest newt, that has been shown to arouse tremendous fear in people who already have (a) a spaghetti phobia, (b) a worm phobia, and (c) mysophobia.

APA CODES: 3.02–3.04

Social Skills Training

Preliminary Measures:

Sociability.

APA CODE: 3.03

The adolescents were divided into 18 groups according to whether they selected a role model who was (1) Black, White, or Cuban, (2) male or female, and (3) an athlete, entertainer, or scientist.

APA CODE: 3.04

Integrative Exercise: Headings and Series

IRRATIONAL FEAR

Fear of Living Organisms

Amphibian Phobias

Fear of salamanders.

Forest newt phobia. There is a salamander found near Salamanca, New York, a tiny pink and white forest newt, that has been shown to arouse tremendous fear in people who already have (1) a spaghetti phobia, (2) a worm phobia, and (3) mysophobia.

APA CODES: 3.02–3.04

Guidelines to Reduce Bias in Language
APA Codes: 3.12–3.17

NOTES:

The participants were asked to think of a favorite teacher from elementary school and to rate her or him on the 20 evaluative dimensions.

APA CODE: 3.12

The experimenter can decide when to provide the debriefing.

APA CODE: 3.12

Typically, the department chair must give approval for each traineeship that is awarded.

APA CODE: 3.12

The effects of social stimuli on eating have been investigated in the rat, monkey, and human.

APA CODE: 3.12

The participants were 20 male students and 20 female students.

APA CODE: 3.12

Each response was rated by a group of men and a group of women.

APA CODE: 3.12

Among the participants were 10 male-to-female transgender persons and 12 female-to-male transgender persons.

APA CODE: 3.12

The male-to-female transsexual had undergone a sex reassignment.

APA CODE: 3.12

A psychological test battery was given to gay men and lesbians and to heterosexual men and women to determine whether there is a relation between childhood sexual abuse and sexual identity.

APA CODE: 3.13

Guidelines to Reduce Bias in Language
APA Codes: 3.12–3.17

These exercises give you practice in using nonsexist language and avoiding ethnic bias (see the *Publication Manual*, sections 3.12–3.17). Mark corrections directly on the right-hand page, and compare your responses with the correct answers on the left-hand page. When you are finished with this section, go on to the next section on which you need practice.

The participants were asked to think of a favorite teacher from elementary school and to rate her on the 20 evaluative dimensions.

APA CODE: 3.12

The experimenter can decide when he should provide the debriefing.

APA CODE: 3.12

Typically, the department chairman must give his approval for each traineeship that is awarded.

APA CODE: 3.12

The effects of social stimuli on eating have been investigated in the rat, monkey, and man.

APA CODE: 3.12

The participants were 20 male students and 20 undergraduate women.

APA CODE: 3.12

Each response was rated by a group of men and a group of females.

APA CODE: 3.12

Among the participants were 10 male-to-female transgenders and 12 female-to-male transgenders.

APA CODE: 3.12

The male-to-female transsexual had undergone a sex change.

APA CODE: 3.12

A psychological test battery was given to gay men and women and to normal men and women to determine whether there is a relation between childhood sexual abuse and sexual identity.

APA CODE: 3.13

The expert judges classified the callers as Black, White, or Asian on the basis of voice characteristics. The researchers then determined the proportion of callers in each group who were urged to seek an abortion.

- ■ ***Note to students:*** The *Publication Manual* offers guidance on terms to use to refer to different racial and ethnic groups; it directs you to find out what the preferred term is and to use it in consideration of your readers. It reminds you to follow two basic guidelines: specificity and sensitivity. We followed the directions of the *Publication Manual* in the use of *Black, White,* and *Asian* in this example; in the terms we identified as correct in other exercises; and in the test items in this instructional guide. Because preferences and styles change over time, it is probably more important that you know to check for the preferred term than that the particular term you use in a given exercise or test item matches our judgment as to the most appropriate term.

APA CODE: 3.14

An attempt was made to compare Native Americans who had been raised on reservations with Native Americans who had been raised in cities.

APA CODE: 3.14

North American children from Los Angeles and Cuban children from Havana were compared in terms of moral development and socialization.

APA CODE: 3.14

The students were interested in research about the mental health needs of children and adolescents with intellectual disabilities.

APA CODE: 3.15

The study described an early intervention program for parents of children with autism.

APA CODE: 3.15

The authors reviewed how popular stereotypes of aging affect the attitudes of older individuals toward certain activities.

APA CODE: 3.16

The regulation of the discrete emotions anger and sadness were examined in adolescents through older adults in the context of describing everyday problem situations.

APA CODE: 3.16

Integrative Exercise: Guidelines to Reduce Bias in Language

College students were randomly assigned to same-sex or cross-sex dyads. After a coffee break, they were asked to rate the etiquette of their partner. The female students rated the female partners higher than they rated the male partners. The male students in this study rated their female partners highly only when the female partners were not assertive (i.e., when they did not initiate social exchanges or change a topic of conversation). However, the lowest etiquette ratings were assigned by the male students to the other male students. Independent observations indicated that the male students were more assertive with the other male students than with the female students but that the female students were more assertive with the other female students than with the male students.

APA CODES: 3.12–3.17

The expert judges classified the callers as Negro, Caucasian, or Oriental on the basis of voice characteristics. The researchers then determined the proportion of callers in each group who were urged to seek an abortion.

APA CODE: 3.14

An attempt was made to compare indians who had been raised on reservations with indians who had been raised in cities.

APA CODE: 3.14

American children from Los Angeles and Hispanic children from Havana were compared in terms of moral development and socialization.

APA CODE: 3.14

The students were interested in research about the mental health needs of retarded children and adolescents.

APA CODE: 3.15

The study described an early intervention program for parents of autistics.

APA CODE: 3.15

The authors reviewed how popular stereotypes of aging affect the attitudes of the elderly toward certain activities.

APA CODE: 3.16

The regulation of the discrete emotions anger and sadness was examined in subjects under 18 years through subjects over 65 years in the context of describing everyday problem situations.

APA CODE: 3.16

Integrative Exercise: Guidelines to Reduce Bias in Language

College students were randomly assigned to same-sex or cross-sex dyads. After a coffee break, they were asked to rate the etiquette of their partner. The undergraduate girls rated the girl partners higher than they the rated male partners. The men in this study rated the girls highly only when the girls were ladylike and not assertive (i.e., when they did not initiate social exchanges or change a topic of conversation). However, the lowest etiquette ratings were assigned by the men to the other guys. Independent observations indicated that the guys acted more masculine with the other guys than with the girls but that the girls were more masculine with the other girls than with the assertive men.

APA CODES: 3.12–3.17

Grammar
APA Codes: 3.18–3.23

NOTES:

Practitioners have experienced the dilemma for years.

APA CODE: 3.18

The experimenter then asked the child to name the object.

APA CODE: 3.18

Results
The social facilitation effect in Experiment 2 replicated our findings in Experiment 1.

APA CODE: 3.18

Schachter and Singer (1962) proposed that emotional states have physiological and cognitive components.
Correct as is.

APA CODE: 3.18

Cognitive psychologists have used the computer metaphor since the 1960s.

APA CODE: 3.18

The leader as well as the group members was asked to perform the second task individually.

APA CODE: 3.19

The criterion for learning was 10 consecutive correct choices.

APA CODE: 3.19

As with most illusory phenomena, this illusion provides an interesting demonstration but generates few experiments.

APA CODE: 3.19

Grammar
APA Codes: 3.18–3.23

In this group of exercises you can practice and learn about verb tense, subject–verb agreement, pronouns, misplaced and dangling modifiers, relative pronouns and subordinate conjunctions, and parallel construction (see the *Publication Manual,* sections 3.18–3.23). Mark corrections directly on the right-hand page, and compare your responses with the correct answers on the left-hand page. When you are finished with this section, go on to the next section on which you need practice.

The dilemma has been experienced by practitioners for years.

APA CODE: 3.18

The experimenter then asks the child to name the object.

APA CODE: 3.18

Results

The social facilitation effect in Experiment 2 replicates our findings in Experiment 1.

APA CODE: 3.18

Schachter and Singer (1962) proposed that emotional states have physiological and cognitive components.

APA CODE: 3.18

Cognitive psychologists used the computer metaphor since the 1960s.

APA CODE: 3.18

The leader as well as the group members were asked to perform the second task individually.

APA CODE: 3.19

The criteria for learning was 10 consecutive correct choices.

APA CODE: 3.19

As with most illusory phenomenon, this illusion provides an interesting demonstration but generates few experiments.

APA CODE: 3.19

The data confirm the inhibitory hypothesis.

APA CODE: 3.19

The moving stimuli were the most effective.

APA CODE: 3.19

After each respondent made a preliminary rating based on the picture, he or she read the detailed information and made a second rating.

APA CODE: 3.20

The clients who achieved a score above the criterion were allowed to participate in the group activity for that day.

APA CODE: 3.20

The group of students who participated in the first experiment were significantly distinct from each other on all motivational scales.

APA CODE: 3.20

A second group of respondents rated, on attractiveness, the person whom the members of the first group selected most frequently as a partner.

APA CODE: 3.20

Using the narrative technique, the raters evaluated the therapists.

APA CODE: 3.21

In the overt condition, the children made a total of only 12 incorrect classifications.

APA CODE: 3.21

The data confirms the inhibitory hypothesis.

APA CODE: 3.19

The moving stimuli was the most effective.

APA CODE: 3.19

After each respondent made a preliminary rating based on the picture, they read the detailed information and made a second rating.

APA CODE: 3.20

The clients that achieved a score above the criterion were allowed to participate in the group activity for that day.

APA CODE: 3.20

The group of students that participated in the first experiment were significantly distinct from each other on all motivational scales.

APA CODE: 3.20

A second group of respondents rated, on attractiveness, the person who the members of the first group selected most frequently as a partner.

APA CODE: 3.20

The raters evaluated the therapists using the narrative technique.

APA CODE: 3.21

In the overt condition, the children only made a total of 12 incorrect classifications.

APA CODE: 3.21

The parent recorded each utterance the child made. After counting the number of utterances, the parent gave the child the appropriate story to read.

APA CODE: 3.21

The format that was easiest to decipher during pilot testing was used during the main part of the experiment.
Correct as is.

APA CODE: 3.22

The training technique that was easiest to administer turned out to be the one that was most effective.

APA CODE: 3.22

Error trials, which were equally frequent in the two conditions, were eliminated from the analysis.

APA CODE: 3.22

Although the group that was returned to the original context made more correct identifications, they also made more false alarms.

APA CODE: 3.22

Behavioral treatments were judged easier to administer by the therapists, and client-centered methods were judged more enjoyable by the clients.

APA CODE: 3.22

Because there were no significant main effects or interactions involving experimenter, the data from the different experimenters were pooled.

APA CODE: 3.22

The parent recorded each utterance the child made. After counting the number of utterances, the child was given the appropriate story to read.

APA CODE: 3.21

The format that was easiest to decipher during pilot testing was used during the main part of the experiment.

APA CODE: 3.22

The training technique which was easiest to administer turned out to be the one that was most effective.

APA CODE: 3.22

Error trials, that were equally frequent in the two conditions, were eliminated from the analysis.

APA CODE: 3.22

While the group that was returned to the original context made more correct identifications, they also made more false alarms.

APA CODE: 3.22

Behavioral treatments were judged easier to administer by the therapists, while client-centered methods were judged more enjoyable by the clients.

APA CODE: 3.22

Since there were no significant main effects or interactions involving experimenter, the data from the different experimenters were pooled.

APA CODE: 3.22

Since the last edition of this text, there has been a major revision in the research paradigms used to explore these phenomena.
Correct as is.

APA CODE: 3.22

The group leader directed that all comments should be positive and that negative ideas should be rephrased as productive suggestions.

APA CODE: 3.23

The judges could not distinguish between the children's drawings of human beings and the children's drawings of other species.

APA CODE: 3.23

The experimenter administered either the drug or a placebo to each participant.

APA CODE: 3.23

It is difficult not only for the computer to solve this problem but also for human beings to solve it.

APA CODE: 3.23

The confederates were told that they should make the first choice, that they should use a neutral evaluation, and that they should avoid making eye contact with the participant.

APA CODE: 3.23

Since the last edition of this text, there has been a major revision in the research paradigms used to explore these phenomena.

APA CODE: 3.22

The group leader directed that all comments should be positive and negative ideas should be rephrased as productive suggestions.

APA CODE: 3.23

The judges could not distinguish between the children's drawings of human beings and other species.

APA CODE: 3.23

The experimenter either administered the drug or a placebo to each participant.

APA CODE: 3.23

It is not only difficult for the computer to solve this problem but also for human beings to solve it.

APA CODE: 3.23

The confederates were told that they should make the first choice, that they should use a neutral evaluation, and to avoid making eye contact with the participant.

APA CODE: 3.23

Integrative Exercise: Grammar

Discussion

Although previous researchers have investigated the gender roles that children develop for their own behaviors, we monitored the gender-based schemata for the behavior of others that young children develop. As we predicted, the gender of the storyteller affected both the children's selection of the story to be read and their overt responses during the reading. The children were more likely to choose stories with action verbs in the titles for the male storyteller to read than for the female storyteller to read. Furthermore, the children were more likely both to leave their seats and to interject comments while the male was reading than while the female was reading. We found the same effects in Experiment 1 with 4-year-olds and in Experiment 2 with 2-year-olds. There was no difference, in either age group, between the expectations exhibited by boys and the expectations exhibited by girls.

The data indicate that gender role expectations develop at a younger age than had been indicated through the use of other response measures. Because neither the storyteller nor the books were familiar to any of the children, it seems reasonable to attribute the findings to a general role expectation rather than to specific experiences with the readers or with the stories. We can be sure that the expectations were the children's and not the observer's because the storyteller, as well as the books, was hidden from the children's observers. In addition, the storytellers' observers detected no differences in verbal or nonverbal cues for action and participation provided by the male and female storytellers whom we recruited and trained. The expectations seem to have wide generality, as the books that the children chose represented diverse topics and characters, and the behavioral differences in listening behaviors were not limited to the children who had selected the stories. As a further test of the generality of the phenomenon, we plan to use the same procedure to investigate children's gender role expectations for other people of varying ages.

APA CODES: 3.18–3.23

Integrative Exercise: Grammar

Discussion

    While previous researchers have investigated the gender roles that children develop for their own behaviors, we monitored the gender-based schemas for the behavior of others which young children develop. As we predicted, the gender of the storyteller affects both the children's selection of the story to be read and their overt responses during the reading. The children were more likely to choose stories with action verbs in the titles for the male storyteller to read than the female storyteller. Furthermore, the children were both more likely to leave their seats and to interject comments while the male was reading than while the female was reading. The same effects were found by us in Experiment 1 with 4-year-olds and in Experiment 2 with 2-year-olds. There was no difference between the expectations exhibited by boys and girls in either age group.

    The data indicates that gender role expectations develop at a younger age than had been indicated through the use of other response measures. Since neither the storyteller nor the books was familiar to any of the children, it seems reasonable to attribute the findings to a general role expectation rather than specific experiences with the readers or the stories. We can be sure that the expectations were the children's and not the observer's because the storyteller as well as the books were hidden from the children's observers. In addition, the storytellers' observers detected no differences in verbal or nonverbal cues for action and participation provided by the male and female storytellers who we recruited and trained. The expectations seem to have wide generality, as the books that the children chose represented diverse topics and characters, and the behavioral differences in listening behaviors were not limited to the children that had selected the stories. As a further test of the generality of the phenomenon, we plan to investigate children's gender role expectations for other people of varying ages using the same procedure.

APA CODES: 3.18–3.23

Punctuation
APA Codes: 4.01–4.11

NOTES:

Laboratory courses in psychology, even at the undergraduate level, cover a variety of substantive topics: learning, memory, cognition, social behavior, individual differences, and physiological psychology.

APA CODE: 4.01

All mathematics teachers know that word problems are more difficult for students to solve than are numerical problems. What the teachers do not know is how to teach students to solve word problems. Correct as is.

APA CODE: 4.02

The selection was translated from English into each of the other five languages. Native speakers of each language, who were also proficient in English, carried out the translations.

APA CODE: 4.02

Speed of recovery after surgery was compared for patients who had a dog at home and for patients who had a cat at home. Patients who had both a dog and a cat were not included in the study.

APA CODE: 4.02

Fathers who were single parents were expected to display greater androgyny than were fathers in dual-parent households. Androgyny was assessed by a standard inventory and by an activity checklist.

APA CODE: 4.02

Average intelligence scores are a defining characteristic of dyslexia. Thus, it is impossible to compare empirically the intelligence of dyslexic and normal-reading children.

APA CODE: 4.02

Punctuation
APA Codes: 4.01–4.11

These exercises cover the use of periods, commas, semicolons, colons, dashes, quotation marks, parentheses, brackets and slashes, as well as correct spacing in typing (see the *Publication Manual*, sections 4.01–4.11). Mark corrections directly on the right-hand page, and compare your responses with the correct answers on the left-hand page. When you are finished with this section, go on to the next section on which you need practice.

Laboratory courses in psychology, even at the undergraduate level, cover a variety of substantive topics: learning, memory, cognition, social behavior, individual differences, and physiological psychology.

APA CODE: 4.01

All mathematics teachers know that word problems are more difficult for students to solve than are numerical problems. What the teachers do not know is how to teach students to solve word problems.

APA CODE: 4.02

The selection was translated from English into each of the other five languages, native speakers of each language, who were also proficient in English, carried out the translations.

APA CODE: 4.02

Speed of recovery after surgery was compared for patients who had a dog at home and for patients who had a cat at home; Patients who had both a dog and a cat were not included in the study.

APA CODE: 4.02

Fathers who were single parents were expected to display greater androgyny than were fathers in dual-parent households, and androgyny was assessed by a standard inventory and by an activity checklist.

APA CODE: 4.02

Average intelligence scores are a defining characteristic of dyslexia—Thus, it is impossible to compare empirically the intelligence of dyslexic and normal-reading children.

APA CODE: 4.02

The child was seated at a table and given a variety of materials to use for the collage.

APA CODE: 4.03

The independent variables were partner's gender, audience size, and criterion for success.

APA CODE: 4.03

Any response that resulted in reward for the contingent participant also resulted in reward for the yoked partner.

APA CODE: 4.03

The computer monitor displayed the training options, and the respondent selected one by pressing the corresponding key.

APA CODE: 4.03

The confederate who was going to agree with the participant always spoke up before the confederate who was going to disagree with the participant.

APA CODE: 4.03

The description of the assault, which was taken from an actual case, was identical for the respondents in all of the experimental conditions.
Correct as is.

APA CODE: 4.03

The possibilities were suggested by Miller, Galanter, and Pribram (1960).
Correct as is.

APA CODE: 4.03

The treatment was tested on clients who complained of phobias or addictions.

APA CODE: 4.03

The team member who scored the highest on the preliminary task was the designated leader.

APA CODE: 4.03

The child was seated at a table, and given a variety of materials to use for the collage.

APA CODE: 4.03

The independent variables were partner's gender, audience size and criterion for success.

APA CODE: 4.03

Any response, that resulted in reward for the contingent participant, also resulted in reward for the yoked partner.

APA CODE: 4.03

The computer monitor displayed the training options and the respondent selected one by pressing the corresponding key.

APA CODE: 4.03

The confederate, who was going to agree with the participant, always spoke up before the confederate, who was going to disagree with the participant.

APA CODE: 4.03

The description of the assault, which was taken from an actual case, was identical for the respondents in all of the experimental conditions.

APA CODE: 4.03

The possibilities were suggested by Miller, Galanter, and Pribram (1960).

APA CODE: 4.03

The treatment was tested on clients who complained of phobias, or addictions.

APA CODE: 4.03

The team member, who scored the highest on the preliminary task, was the designated leader.

APA CODE: 4.03

Pupillary dilation was measured at the time of stimulus onset; heart rate was measured when the response was emitted.

APA CODE: 4.04

Respondents were told that the occupations of the three people were newscaster, farmer, and accountant; teacher, plumber, and dentist; or optician, librarian, and welder.

APA CODE: 4.04

The same speech confusions have been reported for bilingual children (Cardozo, 1984; Nakamura & Kato, 1978; Rivera, Mendez, & Avila, 1985).
Correct as is.

APA CODE: 4.04

Expertise has been investigated in chess playing (Charness, 1981; Chase & Simon, 1973).

APA CODE: 4.04

The essays that the first group read were student generated; those that the second group read were computer generated.
Correct as is.

APA CODE: 4.04

The different methodologies have resulted in the same outcome: Constraining the alternatives results in faster solutions but poorer transfer.

APA CODE: 4.05

For the three types of training, the proportions of new:old solutions were 1:3, 1:7, and 1:20, respectively.
Correct as is.

APA CODE: 4.05

The order of preference for partners was as follows: adult-female, child-female, child-male, and adult-male.

APA CODE: 4.05

Pupillary dilation was measured at the time of stimulus onset, heart rate was measured when the response was emitted.

APA CODE: 4.04

Respondents were told that the occupations of the three people were newscaster, farmer, and accountant, teacher, plumber, and dentist, or optician, librarian, and welder.

APA CODE: 4.04

The same speech confusions have been reported for bilingual children (Cardozo, 1984; Nakamura & Kato, 1978; Rivera, Mendez, & Avila, 1985).

APA CODE: 4.04

Expertise has been investigated in chess playing (Charness, 1981, Chase & Simon, 1973).

APA CODE: 4.04

The essays that the first group read were student generated; those that the second group read were computer generated.

APA CODE: 4.04

The different methodologies have resulted in the same outcome—constraining the alternatives results in faster solutions but poorer transfer.

APA CODE: 4.05

For the three types of training, the proportions of new:old solutions were 1:3, 1:7, and 1:20, respectively.

APA CODE: 4.05

The order of preference for partners was as follows: Adult-female, child-female, child-male, and adult-male.

APA CODE: 4.05

The different immigrant groups—European Jews, Hispanic Catholics, and Asian Buddhists—have displayed different forms of assimilation.

APA CODE: 4.06

The participants rated their judgments on a 5-point scale ranging from *just guessing* to *absolutely certain.*

APA CODE: 4.07

He clarified the distinction between *farther* and *further.*

APA CODE: 4.07

The term *multivariate analysis* is reserved for investigations that use multiple dependent variables.

APA CODE: 4.07

An attempt was made to breed "vagabond" rats by inbreeding in each succeeding generation those rats that relocated their nests most frequently. Relocation behavior was assessed in each of 12 successive inbred generations of vagabond rats and control rats.
Correct as is.

APA CODE: 4.07

The article by Brown and Kulik (1977), "Flashbulb Memories," contains reports of powerful naturalistic memories.

APA CODE: 4.07

Miele (1993) found that "the placebo effect, which had been verified in previous studies, disappeared when [only the first group's] behaviors were studied in this manner" (p. 276).

APA CODE: 4.08

The "placebo effect," which had been verified in previous studies, disappeared when behaviors were studied in this manner. Furthermore, the behaviors *were never exhibited again* [italics added], even when reel [*sic*] drugs were administered. Earlier studies (e.g., Abdullah, 1984; Fox, 1979) were clearly premature in attributing the results to a placebo effect. (p. 276)

APA CODE: 4.08

Garcia and Koelling (1966) demonstrated prepared learning.

APA CODE: 4.09

Need achievement was assessed using the Thematic Apperception Test (TAT).

APA CODE: 4.09

The different immigrant groups, European Jews, Hispanic Catholics, and Asian Buddhists, have displayed different forms of assimilation.

APA CODE: 4.06

The participants rated their judgments on a 5-point scale ranging from "just guessing" to "absolutely certain."

APA CODE: 4.07

He clarified the distinction between "farther" and "further."

APA CODE: 4.07

The term "multivariate analysis" is reserved for investigations that use multiple dependent variables.

APA CODE: 4.07

An attempt was made to breed "vagabond" rats by inbreeding in each succeeding generation those rats that relocated their nests most frequently. Relocation behavior was assessed in each of 12 successive inbred generations of vagabond rats and control rats.

APA CODE: 4.07

The article by Brown and Kulik (1977), *Flashbulb Memories*, contains reports of powerful naturalistic memories.

APA CODE: 4.07

Miele (1993) found that "the "placebo effect," which had been verified in previous studies, disappeared when [only the first group's] behaviors were studied in this manner" (p. 276).

APA CODE: 4.08

"The 'placebo effect,' which had been verified in previous studies, disappeared when behaviors were studied in this manner. Furthermore, the behaviors *were never exhibited again* [italics added], even when reel [*sic*] drugs were administered. Earlier studies (e.g., Abdullah, 1984; Fox, 1979) were clearly premature in attributing the results to a placebo effect (p. 276)."

APA CODE: 4.08

Garcia and Koelling, 1966, demonstrated prepared learning.

APA CODE: 4.09

Need achievement was assessed using the Thematic Apperception Test, TAT.

APA CODE: 4.09

The distribution of reaction times was skewed. (Error responses, which accounted for less than 1% of the responses, were eliminated from this and all subsequent analyses.)

APA CODE: 4.09

Although there was an effect for adolescent girls (see Table 1), the effect was greater for adolescent boys (see Table 2).

APA CODE: 4.09

The three types of observers were (a) parents of the children being observed, (b) parents of matched children who were not being observed, and (c) childless adults who were matched on age with the parents of the children being observed.

APA CODE: 4.09

(Brown, 2008, used a similar paradigm.)
Correct as is.

APA CODE: 4.10

The test–retest reliability was assessed by a three-layered approach which consisted of Pearson product– moment correlation, analysis of variance (ANOVA), and standard error of measurement (SEM).

APA CODE: 4.11

The distribution of reaction times was skewed. (Error responses, which accounted for less than 1% of the responses, were eliminated from this and all subsequent analyses).

APA CODE: 4.09

Although there was an effect for adolescent girls (see Table 1,) the effect was greater for adolescent boys (see Table 2.)

APA CODE: 4.09

The three types of observers were a: parents of the children being observed, b: parents of matched children who were not being observed, and c: childless adults who were matched on age with the parents of the children being observed.

APA CODE: 4.09

(Brown, 2008, used a similar paradigm.)

APA CODE: 4.10

The test/retest reliability was assessed by a three-layered approach which consisted of Pearson product/moment correlation, analysis of variance (ANOVA), and standard error of measurement (SEM).

APA CODE: 4.11

Integrative Exercise: Punctuation

Each participant performed three tasks—a memory-span test, an analogies test, and a syllogistic-reasoning test—during the experimental session. The memory-span task was presented orally, and the other two tasks were presented in written form. The memory task was always given first, followed by the analogies and reasoning tasks in counterbalanced order. Thus, the tasks were given in one of two orders: memory, analogies, and reasoning or memory, reasoning, and analogies. Four different contents were used for the tasks: abstract, "little-boy" thematic, "little-girl" thematic, and neutral thematic (on the basis of the ratings of topics in Experiment 1). Each participant received the same type of content for all four tasks. Different groups of male and female participants received the four different types of content. The participants were given unlimited time to perform each task; both latency and accuracy of response were recorded for each task. Variations in content were expected to affect performance on all three tasks and to affect the differences between the performance of men and women on the tasks.

APA CODES: 4.01–4.11

Integrative Exercise: Punctuation

Each participant performed three tasks: a memory-span test, an analogies test and a syllogistic-reasoning test, during the experimental session. The memory-span task was presented orally; and the other two tasks were presented in written form. The memory task was always given first. Followed by the analogies and reasoning tasks in counterbalanced order. Thus, the tasks were given in one of two orders: memory, analogies, and reasoning: or memory, reasoning, and analogies. Four different contents were used for the tasks: abstract; little-boy thematic; little-girl thematic; and neutral thematic. (On the basis of the ratings of topics in Experiment 1.). Each participant received the same type of content for all four tasks. Different groups of male, and female, participants received the four different types of content. The participants were given unlimited time to perform each task—both latency and accuracy of response were recorded for each task. Variations in content were expected to affect performance on all three tasks, and to affect the differences between the performance of men and women on the tasks.

APA CODES: 4.01–4.11

Spelling and Hyphenation
APA Codes: 4.12–4.13

NOTES:

Left-handed players were more accurate than right-handed players.

APA CODES: 4.12–4.13

The program simulated the error-producing decisions of novices.
Correct as is.

APA CODES: 4.12–4.13

Temporal groupings were more effective than spatial groupings.

APA CODES: 4.12–4.13

A largely ignored illusion is now receiving attention from researchers.

APA CODES: 4.12–4.13

Blood pressure readings were taken before and after each relaxation session.

APA CODES: 4.12–4.13

The volunteers devoted time each day to skills relevant to job seeking.

APA CODES: 4.12–4.13

The neighborhoods selected contained single- and double-family dwellings.

APA CODES: 4.12–4.13

The experimental design allowed us to assess the effect of the pretest on performance.

APA CODES: 4.12–4.13

An indirect measure of attitude or memory presents fewer opportunities for subjective bias than does self-report.
Correct as is.

APA CODES: 4.12–4.13

Spelling and Hyphenation
APA Codes: 4.12–4.13

These exercises cover spelling and hyphenation (see the *Publication Manual*, sections 4.12–4.13). Mark corrections directly on the right-hand page, and compare your responses with the correct answers on the left-hand page. When you are finished with this section, go on to the next section, go on which you need practice.

Left handed players were more accurate than right handed players.

APA CODES: 4.12–4.13

The program simulated the error-producing decisions of novices.

APA CODES: 4.12–4.13

Temporal-groupings were more effective than spatial-groupings.

APA CODES: 4.12–4.13

A largely-ignored illusion is now receiving attention from researchers.

APA CODES: 4.12–4.13

Blood pressure readings were taken before-and-after each relaxation session.

APA CODES: 4.12–4.13

The volunteers devoted time each day to skills relevant to job-seeking.

APA CODES: 4.12–4.13

The neighborhoods selected contained single and double-family dwellings.

APA CODES: 4.12–4.13

The experimental design allowed us to assess the effect of the pre-test on performance.

APA CODES: 4.12–4.13

An indirect measure of attitude or memory presents fewer opportunities for subjective bias than does self-report.

APA CODES: 4.12–4.13

Integrative Exercise: Spelling and Hyphenation

Memory for unusual foreign words and their English definitions as paired associates was improved using either the peg-word system or key-word system with imagery-arousing instructions. Other, more easily applied mnemonic systems such as the concrete-imagery or the action-imagery system were not tested. Same-sex pairs of sixth graders were randomly assigned to the experimental conditions. In a repeated measures design, children were provided with peg words and key words. Presentations were self-paced. Memory for the to-be-remembered vocabulary items was tested immediately and on a delayed posttest.

APA CODES: 4.12–4.13

Integrative Exercise: Spelling and Hyphenation

Memory for unusual foreign words and their English definitions as paired-associates was improved using either the peg word system or key-word system with imagery-arousing instructions. Other, more-easily applied mnemonic systems such as the concrete imagery or the action-imagery system were not tested. Same-sex pairs of sixth-graders were randomly assigned to the experimental conditions. In a repeated-measures design, children were provided with peg-words and key-words. Presentations were self paced. Memory for the to be remembered vocabulary items was tested immediately and on a delayed post-test.

APA CODES: 4.12–4.13

Capitalization
APA Codes: 2.04, 4.14–4.20

NOTES:

Research supports one conclusion: Cockroaches will avoid or escape bright light.

APA CODE: 4.14

In an article by Pyro and Mani, "A Theory of Firesetting in Children and Adolescents," the authors suggested that fire setting should be studied as a legitimate problem in its own right.

APA CODE: 4.15

The author suggested that Freudian slips can be a symptom of a neurological disorder.
Correct as is.

APA CODE: 4.16

The theory of intrinsic job satisfaction of Hackman and Oldham (1980) describes principles of job redesign.

APA CODE: 4.16

A Sony 2400 portable videocamera was used to record the nonverbal behaviors of students in the love-lie and used-car-lie conditions.

APA CODE: 4.16

Running head: SOCIAL DISTANCE

2

Abstract

In past research, it has been observed that strangers walk closer to physically healthy than to physically impaired persons.
Correct as is.

APA CODE: 2.04

Capitalization
APA Codes: 2.04, 4.14–4.20

These exercises cover the capitalization of (a) words beginning a sentence; (b) major words in titles and headings; (c) proper nouns and trade names; (d) nouns followed by numbers or letters; (e) titles of tests; (f) names of conditions or groups in an experiment; and (g) names of factors, variables, and effects (see the *Publication Manual*, sections 2.04 and 4.14–4.20). Mark corrections directly on the right-hand page, and compare your responses with the correct answers on the left-hand page. When you are finished with this section, go on to the next section on which you need practice.

Research supports one conclusion: cockroaches will avoid or escape bright light.

APA CODE: 4.14

In an article by Pyro and Mani, "A theory of firesetting in children and adolescents," the authors suggested that fire setting should be studied as a legitimate problem in its own right.

APA CODE: 4.15

The author suggested that Freudian slips can be a symptom of a neurological disorder.

APA CODE: 4.16

The Theory of Intrinsic Job Satisfaction of Hackman and Oldham (1980) describes principles of job redesign.

APA CODE: 4.16

A sony 2400 portable videocamera was used to record the nonverbal behaviors of students in the love-lie and used-car-lie conditions.

APA CODE: 4.16

Running head: SOCIAL DISTANCE

2

Abstract

In past research, it has been observed that strangers walk closer to physically healthy than to physically impaired persons.

APA CODE: 2.04

Integrative Exercise: Capitalization

Deudodder (1999), in his article "Time Vacuum Effects and Procrastination in College Students," claimed that many college students suffer from a form of jet lag. In the three studies he reported, Deudodder showed how the typical college student disrupts his or her circadian rhythm without flying on a jet. His "all-nighter-napper" theory suggests that jet lag is produced when students stay awake all night (studying or partying) and then nap the entire following day. To test his theory, he conducted four experiments. In Experiment 1, he asked students from psychology courses to complete the Deudodder Intrazone Time Inventory.

APA CODES: 2.04, 4.14–4.20

Integrative Exercise: Capitalization

Deudodder (1999), in his article "Time vacuum effects and procrastination in college students," claimed that many College students suffer from a form of Jet Lag. In the three studies he reported, Deudodder showed how the typical college student disrupts his or her Circadian rhythm without flying on a jet. His "All-Nighter-Napper" theory suggests that Jet Lag is produced when students stay awake all night (studying or partying) and then nap the entire following day. To test his theory, he conducted four experiments. In experiment 1, he asked students from Psychology courses to complete the Deudodder intrazone time inventory.

APA CODES: 2.04, 4.14–4.20

Italics
APA Code: 4.21

NOTES:

Kelley, in his article in the *American Psychologist*, described three dimensions of causal attribution.

APA CODE: 4.21

Fabricated legal descriptions, called *case facts*, were presented to mock juries; however, case facts were not presented to shadow juries.

APA CODE: 4.21

Children who were low achievers and had low socioeconomic status were rated significantly less competent by their teachers, $F(2, 14) = 7.47$, $p < .001$.

APA CODE: 4.21

Adults who were sensitive to NaCl were also more likely to have hypertension.

APA CODE: 4.21

Genetic theories of psychopathology such as the diathesis stress model suggest that schizophrenia may be predisposed by genetic structures but will not appear without a stressful environment.

APA CODE: 4.21

Integrative Exercise: Italics

A temperature discrimination task was presented to human beings *(Homo sapiens)* and crickets *(Gryllidae)*. Then, just noticeable differences (JNDs) were determined for each species. The JNDs for crickets were smaller, as indicated by a *t* test, than those for human beings.

APA CODE: 4.21

Italics
APA Code: 4.21

These exercises cover the use of italics (see the *Publication Manual*, section 4.21). Mark corrections directly on the right-hand page, and compare your responses with the correct answers on the left-hand page. When you are finished with this section, go on to the next section on which you need practice.

Kelley, in his article in the American Psychologist, described three dimensions of causal attribution.

APA CODE: 4.21

Fabricated legal descriptions, called *case facts*, were presented to mock juries; however, *case facts* were not presented to shadow juries.

APA CODE: 4.21

Children who were low achievers and had low socioeconomic status were rated significantly less competent by their teachers, F(2, 14) = 7.47, p < .001.

APA CODE: 4.21

Adults who were sensitive to *NaCl* were also more likely to have hypertension.

APA CODE: 4.21

Genetic theories of psychopathology such as the diathesis stress model suggest that schizophrenia may be predisposed by genetic structures but will not appear *without* a stressful environment.

APA CODE: 4.21

Integrative Exercise: Italics

A temperature discrimination task was presented to human beings (*Homo sapiens*) and crickets (Gryllidae). Then, just noticeable differences (*JNDs*) were determined for each species. The *JNDs* for crickets were *smaller*, as indicated by a t test, than those for human beings.

APA CODE: 4.21

Abbreviations
APA Codes: 4.22–4.30

NOTES:

According to Steinberg (1985), current measures of IQ do not reflect the triarchic nature of human intelligence.
Correct as is.

APA CODE: 4.24

When the experimenter delivered the conditioned stimulus (CS), the pigeon pecked the key and avoided being drenched in cold water.

APA CODE: 4.25

The reaction time (RT) was recorded after each dolphin received two clicks. The RT was not recorded when killer whales were within sonar range.
Correct as is.

APA CODE: 4.25

Participatory management (e.g., shared goal-setting and mutual evaluation) was more effective in the smaller organizations (i.e., those with fewer than 100 workers).

APA CODE: 4.26

Not all traditional sex role expectancies (e.g., women may cry, men should not cry) transfer into all organizational cultures (i.e., an organization's social environment). Some organizations punish traditional sex role behavior in women but not in men (e.g., military or industrial organizations).

APA CODE: 4.26

It took the respondents 20 s to 2 min to recall the stimulus word. After a 3-hr delay, respondents began the trials again.

APA CODE: 4.27

Abbreviations
APA Codes: 4.22–4.30

These exercises cover the use of abbreviations, explanation of abbreviations, abbreviations accepted as words, abbreviations used often in APA journals, abbreviations of units of measurement and statistics, use of periods with abbreviations, plurals of abbreviations, and abbreviations beginning a sentence (see the *Publication Manual,* sections 4.22–4.30). Mark corrections directly on the right-hand page, and compare your responses with the correct answers on the left-hand page. When you are finished with this section, go on to the next section on which you need practice.

According to Steinberg (1985), current measures of IQ do not reflect the triarchic nature of human intelligence.

APA CODE: 4.24

When the E delivered the CS, the pigeon pecked the key and avoided being drenched in cold water.

APA CODE: 4.25

The reaction time (RT) was recorded after each dolphin received two clicks. The RT was not recorded when killer whales were within sonar range.

APA CODE: 4.25

Participatory management (for example, shared goal-setting and mutual evaluation) was more effective in the smaller organizations (that is, those with fewer than 100 workers).

APA CODE: 4.26

Not all traditional sex role expectancies e.g., women may cry, men should not cry, transfer into all organizational cultures i.e., an organization's social environment. Some organizations punish traditional sex role behavior in women but not in men e.g., military or industrial organizations.

APA CODE: 4.26

It took the respondents 20 seconds to 2 minutes to recall the stimulus word. After a 3-hour delay, respondents began the trials again.

APA CODE: 4.27

Integrative Exercise: Abbreviations

Fewer abbreviation identification errors were made by readers of papers about learning and memory written in APA Style than in any other writing style. Abbreviations such as intertrial interval (ITI), conditioned stimulus (CS), and short-term memory (STM) were correctly identified by BS and BA students alike regardless of their IQs.

■ *Note to students:* Many of you probably knew that the abbreviations ITI, CS, and STM given in the draft version should have been defined on first use. However, you may not have known what all of the abbreviations stood for, so you could not provide the complete correction. We could think of no better way to make the point that abbreviations must be defined for the reader.

APA CODES: 4.22–4.30

Integrative Exercise: Abbreviations

Fewer abbreviation identification errors were made by readers of papers about learning and memory written in APA Style than in any other writing style. Abbreviations such as ITI, CS, and STM were correctly identified by B.S. and B.A. students alike regardless of their intelligence quotients (IQs).

APA CODES: 4.22–4.30

Quotations
APA Codes: 4.08, 6.03–6.09

NOTES:

The respondent asked, "Is this my or her heartbeat I am hearing?" The experimenter replied, "It is not yours or hers!"
Correct as is.

APA CODE: 4.08

One college student interviewed said, "Campus 'lingo' is not just language, it is a fence to hold in friends and keep out geeks."

APA CODE: 4.08

Dykens and Gerrard (1986) concluded that the psychological profile of bulimics and repeat dieters is similar:

It appears that both repeat dieters and bulimics can be characterized as having low self-esteem and an external locus of control. This profile supports suggestions from case studies that women with eating disorders suffer from feelings of ineffectiveness and lack of control over life decisions. (p. 288)

APA CODE: 6.03

The author speculated that "negative exemplars within the self-concept are more confidently known than affirmative exemplars" (Brinthaup, 1983, p. 52).
Correct as is.

APA CODE: 6.03

These investigators suggested that "although state and trait anxiety appear to have a similar effect on rumor transmission, it cannot be concluded that this effect was produced by similar social processes" (Walker & Beckerle, 1987, p. 358).
Correct as is

APA CODE: 6.03

Four score and seven years ago our fathers brought forth upon this continent a new nation . . . dedicated to the proposition that all men are created equal."

APA CODE: 6.08

Quotations
APA Codes: 4.08, 6.03–6.09

These exercises cover quoting sources, accuracy, double versus single quotation marks, changes from the source requiring no explanation, changes from the source requiring explanation, citation of sources, and permission to quote (see the *Publication Manual*, sections 4.08 and 6.03–6.09). Mark corrections directly on the right-hand page, and compare your responses with the correct answers on the left-hand page. When you are finished with this section, go on to the next section on which you need practice.

The respondent asked, "Is this my or her heartbeat I am hearing?" The experimenter replied, "It is not yours or hers!"

APA CODE: 4.08

One college student interviewed said, "Campus "lingo" is not just another language, it is a fence to hold in friends and keep out geeks."

APA CODE: 4.08

Dykens and Gerrard (1986, p. 288) concluded that the psychological profile of bulimics and repeat dieters is similar: "It appears that both repeat dieters and bulimics can be characterized as having low self-esteem and an external locus of control. This profile supports suggestions from case studies that women with eating disorders suffer from feelings of ineffectiveness and lack of control over life decisions."

APA CODE: 6.03

The author speculated that "negative exemplars within the self-concept are more confidently known than affirmative exemplars" (Brinthaup, 1983, p. 52).

APA CODE: 6.03

These investigators suggested that "although state and trait anxiety appear to have a similar effect on rumor transmission, it cannot be concluded that this effect was produced by similar social processes" (Walker & Beckerle, 1987, p. 358).

APA CODE: 6.03

"Four score and seven years ago our fathers brought forth upon this continent a new nation. . . . dedicated to the proposition that all men are created equal."

APA CODE: 6.08

Integrative Exercise: Quotations

Duerf (1990) suggested that "the 'subliminal guilt effect' happens only when semi-nude images are subtly inscribed on the labels of whiskey bottles of light drinkers" (p. 68). Duerf concluded the following:

Some light drinkers have a negative oral fixation which inhibits their pursuit of oral pleasure.

One ounce of alcohol from the forbidden bottle apparently releases a flood of libido associated

with the mouth *and* the genitals. Oral guilt enters through the front door and sexual guilt

sneaks in the back like an *uninvited* [italics added] guest. (p. 101)

APA CODES: 4.08, 6.03–6.09

Integrative Exercise: Quotations

Duerf (1990) suggested that "the "subliminal guilt effect" happens only when semi-nude images are subtly inscribed on the labels of whiskey bottles of light drinkers (p. 68)". Duerf concluded the following:

> Some light drinkers have a negative oral fixation which inhibits their pursuit of oral pleasure. One ounce of alcohol from the forbidden bottle apparently releases a flood of libido associated with the mouth *and* the genitals. Oral guilt enters through the front door and sexual guilt sneaks in the back like an *uninvited* [italics added] guest, (page 101)

APA CODES: 4.08, 6.03–6.09

Reference Citations in Text
APA Codes: 6.05, 6.11–6.21

NOTES:

Basu and Jones (2007, para. 4) go so far as to suggest the need for a new intellectual framework in which to consider the nature and form of regulation in cyberspace.

APA CODES: 6.05, 6.19

The concept of chunking was introduced by Miller (1956).

APA CODE: 6.11

Play has an important role in children's brain development (Henig, 2008).

APA CODE: 6.11

Sternberg (1966) was the first to report the effect of target set size on reaction time. Sternberg used target sets of size 1, 2, or 4.

APA CODE: 6.11

Kenney and Gould (2008) studied the effects of nicotine on fear learning, building on the work of Gould and Wehner (1999) on nicotine and contextual fear conditioning. Kenney and Gould administered nicotine prior to contextual learning and also prior to context-shock associative learning.

APA CODE: 6.12

Arnau, Rosen, Finch, Rhudy, and Fortunato (2007) tested the effects of two components of hope, Agency and Pathways, on depression and anxiety. Similar studies have used the same conceptualization of hope to test, for example, its effects on mental and physical health (Magaletta & Oliver, 1999). Arnau et al. found that hope is negatively associated with depression and anxiety. Correct as is.

APA CODE: 6.12

Reference Citations in Text
APA Codes: 6.05, 6.11–6.21

These exercises give you practice in citing in text works by a single author, by two or more authors, by corporate authors, with no author or with an anonymous author, by authors with the same surname, and by two or more authors within the same set of parentheses; specific parts of a source; personal communications; references to legal materials; and references in parenthetical material (see the *Publication Manual,* sections 6.05 and 6.11–6.21). Mark corrections directly on the right-hand page, and compare your responses with the correct answers on the left-hand page. When you are finished with this section, go on to the next section on which you need practice.

Basu and Jones (para. 4, 2007) go so far as to suggest the need for a new intellectual framework in which to consider the nature and form of regulation in cyberspace.

APA CODES: 6.05, 6.19

The concept of chunking was introduced by Miller (Miller, 1956).

APA CODE: 6.11

Play has an important role in children's brain development (Henig, *The New York Times Magazine*, 2008).

APA CODE: 6.11

Sternberg (1966) was the first to report the effect of target set size on reaction time. Sternberg (1966) used target sets of size 1, 2, or 4.

APA CODE: 6.11

Kenney & Gould (2008) studied the effects of nicotine on fear learning, building on the work of Gould & Wehner (1999) on nicotine and contextual fear conditioning. Kenney et al. administered nicotine prior to contextual learning and also prior to context-shock associative learning.

APA CODE: 6.12

Arnau, Rosen, Finch, Rhudy, and Fortunato (2007) tested the effects of two components of hope, Agency and Pathways, on depression and anxiety. Similar studies have used the same conceptualization of hope to test, for example, its effects on mental and physical health (Magaletta & Oliver, 1999). Arnau et al. found that hope is negatively associated with depression and anxiety.

APA CODE: 6.12

Diaz-Guerrero, Reyes-Lagunes, Witzke, and Holtzman (1976) investigated the effects of TV in a different culture. Diaz-Guerrero et al. used an experimental design with randomization to demonstrate the effectiveness of watching "Sesame Street" among Mexican preschool children.

APA CODE: 6.12

The Dispositional Hope Scale (DHS; Snyder et al., 1991) consists of two subsets of items measuring Agency and Pathways.

APA CODE: 6.12

One research question that attempted to address the larger issue was whether a difference in presenting symptoms of schizophrenia existed among ethnic Malay, Chinese, and Indian patients (Ainsah, Nurulwafa, & Osman, 2008).

APA CODE: 6.12

Immunocompromized travelers should check before getting vaccines for typhoid, yellow fever, and other diseases, as some of these vaccines may be contraindicated (Centers for Disease Control and Prevention, 2007, Chapter 9).

APA CODES: 6.13, 6.19

An early example of computer simulation of human problem-solving performance is the General Problem-Solver (Newell, Shaw, & Simon, 1959; Newell & Simon, 1961, 1972).

APA CODE: 6.16

What has been demonstrated at the level of electrophysiological recordings is that Wulst neurons are responsive to visual stimuli (Periŝsić, Mihailović, & Cuénod, 1971; Revzin, 1969).

APA CODE: 6.16

Diaz-Guerrero, Reyes-Lagunes, Witzke, and Holtzman (Diaz-Guerrero et al., 1976) investigated the effects of TV in a different culture. Diaz-Guerrero, Reyes-Lagunes, Witzke, and Holtzman used an experimental design with randomization to demonstrate the effectiveness of watching "Sesame Street" among Mexican preschool children.

APA CODE: 6.12

The Dispositional Hope Scale (DHS; Snyder, Harris, Anderson, Holleran, Irving, Sigmon, et al., 1991) consists of two subsets of items measuring Agency and Pathways.

APA CODE: 6.12

One research question that attempted to address the larger issue was whether a difference in presenting symptoms of schizophrenia existed among ethnic Malay, Chinese, and Indian patients (Ainsah, Nurulwafa, Osman, 2008).

APA CODE: 6.12

Immunocompromized travelers should check before getting vaccines for typhoid, yellow fever, and other diseases, as some of these vaccines may be contraindicated (Centers for Disease Control and Prevention, 2007)(chap. 9).

APA CODES: 6.13, 6.19

An early example of computer simulation of human problem-solving performance is the General Problem-Solver (Newell Shaw, & Simon, 1959; Newell & Simon, 1961; Newell & Simon, 1972).

APA CODE: 6.16

What has been demonstrated at the level of electrophysiological recordings is that Wulst neurons are responsive to visual stimuli (Revzin, 1969; Periŝsić, Mihailović, & Cuénod, 1971).

APA CODE: 6.16

Integrative Exercise: Reference Citations in Text

Research on the effects of media violence has a long tradition. Studies that address unspecific physiological arousal effects, now considered a somewhat simplistic conceptualization of emotional effects, has come under heavy criticism (Cacioppo, Berntson, & Crites, 1996; Reisenzein, 1983). Most studies also address behavioral effects of media violence, especially the effects on aggressive behavior (Murray, 2003). In contrast, emotional effects (other than effects on fear) have not been systematically addressed thus far (Wirth & Schramm, 2005).

Most research on media violence has been on fictional media, such as action movies or computer games (e.g., Bryant & Vorderer, 2006), whose primary goals are to entertain the audience and spark our emotions. According to Frijda's (2007) "law of apparent reality," emotions are primarily triggered by events that are evaluated as real, which is why one expects that emotional effects should be stronger when watching nonfictional genres such as TV news. However, it has been shown that watching the news can be, in and of itself, an entertainment and social activity (McQuail, 2001). Furthermore, content analysis shows violence to be an important issue in TV news (Winterhoff-Spurk, 1998; Winterhoff-Spurk, Unz, & Schwab, 2005). Thus, it seems reasonable to pay closer attention to the emotional effects of violent TV news.

APA CODES: 6.05, 6.11–6.21

Integrative Exercise: Reference Citations in Text

Research on the effects of media violence has a long tradition. Studies that address unspecific physiological arousal effects, now considered a somewhat simplistic conceptualization of emotional effects, have come under heavy criticism (Reisenzein, 1983, Cacioppo, Berntson, & Crites, 1996). Most studies also address behavioral effects of media violence, especially the effects on aggressive behavior (Murray, 2003). In contrast, emotional effects (other than effects on fear) have not been systematically addressed thus far (Wirth and Schramm, 2005).

Most research on media violence has been on fictional media, such as action movies or computer games, for example, that of Bryant and Vorderer, 2006, whose primary goals are to entertain the audience and spark our emotions. According to Frijda's 2007 "law of apparent reality," emotions are primarily triggered by events that are evaluated as real, which is why one expects that emotional effects should be stronger when watching nonfictional genres such as TV news. However, it has been shown that watching the news can be, in and of itself, an entertainment and social activity (McQuail, 2001). Furthermore, content analysis shows violence to be an important issue in TV news (Winterhoff-Spurk, Unz & Schwab, 2005; Winterhoff-Spurk, 1998). Thus, it seems reasonable to pay closer attention to the emotional effects of violent TV news.

APA CODES: 6.05, 6.11–6.21

Reference List
APA Codes: 6.22–6.25, 7.01–7.11, Appendix 7.1

NOTES:

Blackwell, E., & Conrod, P. J. (2003). *A five-dimensional measure of drinking motives.* Unpublished manuscript, Department of Psychology, University of British Columbia, Canada.
Correct as is.
APA CODE: 6.22

Berry, J. W., Poortinga, Y. H., Segall, M. H., & Dasen, P. R. (2002). *Cross-cultural psychology: Research and applications* (2nd ed.). New York, NY: Cambridge University Press.
Berry, J. W., & Sam, D. (1997). Acculturation and adaptation. In J. W. Berry, M. H. Segall, & C. Kagitcibasi (Eds.), *Handbook of cross-cultural psychology: Vol. 3. Social behavior and applications* (pp. 291–326). Boston, MA: Allyn & Bacon.
APA CODE: 6.25

Kazdin, A. E. (2008a). Evidence-based treatment and delivery of psychological services: Shifting our emphases to increase impact. *Psychological Services. 5,* 201–215. doi:10.1037/a0012573
Kazdin, A. E. (2008b). Evidence-based treatment and practice: New opportunities to bridge clinical research and practice, enhance the knowledge base, and improve patient care. *American Psychologist, 63,* 146–159. doi:10.1037/0003-066X.63.3.146
APA CODE: 6.25

Adams, D. K., Mowrer, O. H., Ammons, R. B., Snygg, D., Butler, J. M., Spence, K. W., . . . University of Kentucky, Department of Psychology. (1954). *Learning theory, personality theory, and clinical research: The Kentucky Symposium.* Hoboken, NJ: Wiley. doi:10.1037/11280-000
Adams, H. F. (1912). *Advertising and its mental laws.* New York, NY: Macmillan. doi:10.1037/10733-000
Correct as is.
APA CODE: 6.25

Reference List
APA Codes: 6.22–6.25, 7.01–7.11, Appendix 7.1

These exercises cover construction of an accurate and complete reference list, references to legal materials, the order of references in the reference list, and applying APA reference style (see the *Publication Manual*, sections 6.22–6.25, 7.01–7.11, and Appendix 7.1). Mark corrections directly on the right-hand page, and compare your responses with the correct answers on the left-hand page. When you are finished with this section, you are ready to take the practice test.

Blackwell, E., & Conrod, P. J. (2003). *A five-dimensional measure of drinking motives.* Unpublished manuscript, Department of Psychology, University of British Columbia, Canada.

APA CODE: 6.22

Berry, J. W., & Sam, D. (1997). Acculturation and adaptation. In J. W. Berry, M. H. Segall, & C. Kagitcibasi (Eds.), *Handbook of cross-cultural psychology: Vol. 3. Social behavior and applications* (pp. 291–326). Boston, MA: Allyn & Bacon.
Berry, J. W., Poortinga, Y. H., Segall, M. H., & Dasen, P. R. (2002). *Cross-cultural psychology: Research and applications* (2nd ed.). New York: Cambridge University Press.

APA CODE: 6.25

Kazdin, A. E. (2008). Evidence-based treatment and delivery of psychological services: Shifting our emphases to increase impact. *Psychological Services. 5,* 201–215. doi:10.1037/a0012573
Kazdin, A. E. (2008). Evidence-based treatment and practice: New opportunities to bridge clinical research and practice, enhance the knowledge base, and improve patient care. *American Psychologist, 63,* 146–159. doi:10.1037/0003-066X.63.3.146

APA CODE: 6.25

Adams, D. K., Mowrer, O. H., Ammons, R. B., Snygg, D., Butler, J. M., Spence, K. W., . . . University of Kentucky, Department of Psychology. (1954). *Learning theory, personality theory, and clinical research: The Kentucky Symposium.* Hoboken, NJ: Wiley. doi:10.1037/11280-000
Adams, H. F. (1912). *Advertising and its mental laws.* New York: Macmillan. doi:10.1037/10733-000

APA CODE: 6.25

Wender, P. H. (1998). Attention-deficit hyperactivity disorder in adults. *Psychiatric Clinics of North America, 21,* 761–774. doi: 10.1016/S0193-953X(05)70039-3

Wender, P. H. (2000). ADHD: Attention-deficit hyperactivity disorder in children and adults. New York, NY: Oxford University Press.

Wender, P. H., Ward, M. F., Reimherr, F. W., & Marchant, B. K. (2000). ADHD in adults [Letter to the editor]. *Journal of the Amercian Academy of Child & Adolescent Psychiatry, 39,* 543. doi: 10.1097/00004583-200005000-00001

APA CODE: 6.25

Corral, I., & Landrine, H. (2008). Acculturation and ethnic-minority health behavior: A test of the operant model. *Health Psychology, 27,* 737–745. doi:10.1037/0278-6133.27.6.737

APA CODE: 7.01

Herbst-Damm, K. L., & Kulik, J. A. (2005). Volunteer support, marital status, and the survival times of terminally ill patients. *Health Psychology, 24,* 225–229. doi:10.1037/0278-6133.24.2.225

APA CODE: 7.01

Liddle, H. A., Rowe, C. L., Dakof, G. A., Henderson, C. E., & Greenbaum, P. E. (2009). Multidimensional family therapy for young adolescent substance abuse: Twelve-month outcomes of a randomized controlled trial. *Journal of Consulting and Clinical Psychology, 77,* 12–25. doi:10.1037/a0014160

APA CODE: 7.01

Paris, R. (2008). "For the dream of being here, one sacrifices . . .": Voices of immigrant mothers in a home visiting program. *American Journal of Orthopsychiatry 78,* 141–151. doi: 10.1037/0002-9432.78.2.141. Correct as is.

APA CODE: 7.01

Von Ledebur, S. C. (2007). Optimizing knowledge transfer by new employees in companies. *Knowledge Management Research & Practice.* Advance online publication. doi:10.1057/palgrave.kmrp.8500141

APA CODE: 7.01

Wender, P. H., Ward, M. F., Reimherr, F. W., & Marchant, B. K. (2000). ADHD in adults [Letter to the editor]. *Journal of the Amercian Academy of Child & Adolescent Psychiatry, 39,* 543. doi: 10.1097/00004583-200005000-00001

Wender, P. H. (2000). ADHD: *Attention-deficit hyperactivity disorder in children and adults.* New York, NY: Oxford University Press.

Wender, P. H. (1998). Attention-deficit hyperactivity disorder in adults. *Psychiatric Clinics of North America, 21,* 761–774. doi: 10.1016/S0193-953X(05)70039-3

APA CODE: 6.25

Corral, I., & Landrine, H. (2008). "Acculturation and Ethnic-Minority Health Behavior: A Test of the Operant Model." *Health Psychology, 27,* 737–745. doi:10.1037/0278-6133.27.6.737

APA CODE: 7.01

Herbst-Damm, K. L., and Kulik, J. A. (2005). Volunteer support, marital status, and the survival times of terminally ill patients. *Health Psychology, 24,* 225–229. doi:10.1037/0278-6133.24.2.225

APA CODE: 7.01

Liddle, H. A., Rowe, C. L., Dakof, G. A., Henderson, C. E., & Greenbaum, P. E. (2009). Multidimensional family therapy for young adolescent substance abuse: Twelve-month outcomes of a randomized controlled trial. *Journal of Consulting and Clinical Psychology, 77,* pp. 12–25. doi:10.1037/a0014160

APA CODE: 7.01

Paris, R. (2008). "For the dream of being here, one sacrifices . . .": Voices of immigrant mothers in a home visiting program. *American Journal of Orthopsychiatry 78,* 141–151. doi: 10.1037/0002-9432.78.2.141

APA CODE: 7.01

Von Ledebur, S. C. (2007). Optimizing knowledge transfer by new employees in companies. *Knowledge Management Research & Practice.* Advance publication. DOI.10.1057/palgrave.kmrp.8500141

APA CODE: 7.01

Six sites meet for comprehensive anti-gang initiative conference. (2006, November/December). *OJJDP News @ a Glance*. Retrieved from http://www.ncjrs.gov/html/ojjdp/news_at_glance/216684/topstory.html

APA CODE: 7.01

Schiraldi, G. R. (2001). *The post-traumatic stress disorder sourcebook: A guide to healing, recovery, and growth* [Adobe Digital Editions version]. doi:10.1036/0071393722.

APA CODE: 7.02

Segerstrom, S. C., & Roach, A. R. (2008). On the physical health benefits of self-enhancement. In E. C. Chang (Ed.), *Self-criticism and self-enhancement: Theory, research, and clinical implications* (pp. 37–54). Washington, DC: American Psychological Association. doi:10.1037/11624-003

APA CODE: 7.02

Strong, E. K., Jr., & Uhrbrock, R. S. (1923). Bibliography on job analysis. In L. Outhwaite (Series Ed.), *Personnel Research Series: Vol. 1. Job analysis and the curriculum* (pp. 140–146). doi:10.1037/10762-000

APA CODE: 7.02

Liu, S. (2005, May). *Defending against business crises with the help of intelligent agent based early warning solutions*. Paper presented at the Seventh International Conference on Enterprise Information Systems, Miami, FL. Abstract retrieved from http://www.iceis.org/iceis2005/abstracts_2005.htm

APA CODE: 7.03

Dirda, M. (2008, August 31). Memento mori [Review of the book *Nothing to be frightened of*, by Julian Barnes]. Retrieved from http://www.washingtonpost.com/wp-dyn/content/article/2008/08/28/AR2008082802898.html

APA CODE: 7.06

Pew Hispanic Center. (2004). *Changing channels and crisscrossing cultures: A survey of Latinos on the news media* [Data file and code book]. Retrieved from http://pewhispanic.org/datasets/
Correct as is.

APA CODE: 7.08

FDA Prescription Drug Advertising Rule, 21 C.F.R. § 202.1 (2006).

APA CODE: Appendix 7.1

Anonymous. (November/December, 2006). Six sites meet for comprehensive anti-gang initiative conference. *OJJDP News @ a Glance.* Retrieved from http://www.ncjrs.gov/html/ojjdp/news_at_glance/216684/topstory.html

APA CODE: 7.01

Schiraldi, G. R. (2001). *The Post-Traumatic Stress Disorder Sourcebook: A Guide to Healing, Recovery, and Growth* [Adobe version]. doi:10.1036/0071393722

APA CODE: 7.02

Segerstrom, S. C., & Roach, A. R. (2008). On the physical health benefits of self-enhancement. In E. C. Chang, Editor, *Self-criticism and self-enhancement: Theory, research, and clinical implications* (pp. 37–54). Washington, DC: American Psychological Association. doi:10.1037/11624-003

APA CODE: 7.02

Strong, E. K., Jr., & Uhrbrock, R. S. (1923). "Bibliography on job analysis" (pp. 140–146). In Outhwaite, L. (Series Ed.), *Personnel Research Series: Vol. 1. Job analysis and the curriculum.* doi: 10.1037/10762-000

APA CODE: 7.02

Liu, S. *Defending against business crises with the help of intelligent agent based early warning solutions.* Paper presented at the Seventh International Conference on Enterprise Information Systems, Miami, Florida, May, 2005. Abstract retrieved January 3, 2007, from http://www.iceis.org/iceis2005/abstracts_2005.htm

APA CODE: 7.03

Dirda, M. (2008). Memento mori [Book review, "Nothing to be frightened of," by Julian Barnes]. Retrieved from http://www.washingtonpost.com/wp-dyn/content/article/2008/08/28/AR2008082802898.html

APA CODE: 7.06

Pew Hispanic Center. (2004). *Changing channels and crisscrossing cultures: A survey of Latinos on the news media* [Data file and code book]. Retrieved from http://pewhispanic.org/datasets/

APA CODE: 7.08

FDA Prescription Drug Advertising Rule, vol. 21 *Code of Federal Regulations* § 202.1 (2006).

APA CODE: Appendix 7.1

Integrative Exercise: Reference List

References

Beehr, T. A., & Bennett, M. M. (2007). Examining retirement from a multi-level perspective. In K. S. Shultz & G. A. Adams (Eds.), *Applied Psychology Series: Aging and work in the 21st century* (pp. 277–302). Mahwah, NJ: Erlbaum.

Beehr, T. A., & Franz, T. M. (1987). The current debate about the meaning of stress. In J. M. Ivancevich & D. C. Ganster (Eds.), *Job stress: From theory to suggestion* (pp. 5–36). Binghamton, NY: Haworth.

De Croon, E. M., Blonk, R. W. B., Van der Bleek, A. J., & Frings-Dresen, M. H. W. (2001). The trucker strain monitor: An occupation-specific questionnaire measuring psychological job strain. *International Archives of Occupational and Environmental Health, 74*, 429–436.

Deery, S. J., Erwin, P. J., Iverson, R. D., & Ambrose, M. L. (1995). The determinants of absenteeism: Evidence from Australian blue-collar employees. *International Journal of Human Resource Management, 6*, 825–848.

de Jonge, J., Reuvers, M. M. E. N., Houtman, I. L. D., & Kompier, M. A. J. (2000). Linear and nonlinear relations between psychosocial job characteristics, subjective outcomes, and sickness absence: Baseline results from SMASH. *Journal of Occupational Health Psychology, 5*, 256–268. doi:10.1037/1076-8998.5.2.256

APA CODES: 6.22–6.25, 7.01–7.11, Appendix 7.1

Integrative Exercise: Reference List

References

Beehr, T. A., & Franz, T. M. (1987). "The current debate about the meaning of stress." In J. M. Ivancevich & D. C. Ganster (Eds.), *Job stress: From theory to suggestion* (5–36). Binghamton: Haworth.

Beehr, T. A., & Bennett, M. M. (2007). Examining retirement from a multi-level perspective. In K. S. Shultz & G. A. Adams (Eds.), *Applied Psychology Series: Aging and work in the 21st century* (pp. 277–302). Mahwah, NJ: Erlbaum.

De Croon, E. M., Blonk, R. W. B., Van der Bleek, A. J., Frings-Dresen, M. H. W. (2001). The trucker strain monitor: An occupation-specific questionnaire measuring psychological job strain. *International Archives of Occupational and Environmental Health, Vol. 74,* 429–436.

Deery, S. J., Erwin, P. J., Iverson, R. D., Ambrose, M. L. (1995). The Determinants of Absenteeism: Evidence From Australian Blue-Collar Employees. *International Journal of Human Resource Management, 6,* 825–848.

de Jonge, J., Reuvers, M. M. E. N., Houtman, I. L. D., Kompier, M. A. J. (2000). Linear and nonlinear relations between psychosocial job characteristics, subjective outcomes, and sickness absence: Baseline results from SMASH. *Journal of Occupational Health Psychology, 5,* 256–268. 10.1037/1076-8998.5.2.256

APA CODES: 6.22–6.25, 7.01–7.11, Appendix 7.1

Term Paper Practice Test

The practice test, formatted like the familiarization test, is designed to (a) assess your level of mastery after completing the exercises, (b) help you decide whether you need to study particular topics in the *Publication Manual* in more depth, (c) help you decide whether to go on to the review exercises, and (d) help you decide whether to take a mastery test. There are two answer sheets at the end of the test, one with blanks for you to write in your answers and the other containing the correct answers. Beside each blank you will find the APA code that corresponds to the number of the section in the *Publication Manual* where you can find the answer to that question. Score your test yourself. If your score is low (i.e., 80% or lower) on the practice test, you should do the review exercises at the end of the term paper unit. If your score is above 80%, you may want to take a mastery test, which your instructor will supply.

TERM PAPER PRACTICE TEST

1. A manuscript title should

   a. use abbreviations wherever possible.
   b. contain at least 30 words.
   c. be fully explanatory when standing alone.
   d. begin with the words *A Study of.*

2. Which characteristic of a manuscript helps readers anticipate key points and track the development of an argument in a study?

   a. voice
   b. verb tense
   c. hypotheses
   d. headings
   e. all of the above

3. Edit the following two levels of headings:

   Amphibian Phobias
   Fear of Forest Newts

   a. leave as is
   b.

   Amphibian Phobias

   Fear of Forest Newts

   c.

   AMPHIBIAN PHOBIAS

   Fear of forest newts

   d.

   Amphibian Phobias

   Fear of Forest Newts

4. Edit the following for the presentation of a series:

The participants were divided into three groups: (1) experts, who had completed at least four courses in computer programming; (2) intermediates, who had completed one course in computer programming and (3) novices, who had no experience in computer programming.

   a. leave as is

   b. The participants were divided into three groups: (a) Experts, who had completed at least four courses in computer programming, (b) Intermediates, who had completed one course in computer programming, and (c) Novices, who had no experience in computer programming,

   c. The participants were divided into three groups: a) experts, who had completed at least four courses in computer programming, b) intermediates, who had completed one course in computer programming, and c) novices, who had no experience in computer programming.

   d. The participants were divided into three groups: (a) experts, who had completed at least four courses in computer programming; (b) intermediates, who had completed one course in computer programming; and (c) novices, who had no experience in computer programming.

5. Continuity in the presentation of ideas can be achieved through

   a. the use of only one type of punctuation.

   b. the use of transitional words.

   c. the use of the full range of punctuation to cue the reader to the pauses, inflections, subordination, and pacing normally heard in speech.

   d. all of the above.

   e. b and c.

6. Which of the following phrases is redundant?

   a. a total of 68 respondents

   b. has been previously found

   c. in close proximity

   d. all of the above

   e. none of the above

7. Colloquial expressions such as *write-up,* approximations of quantity such as *quite* a *large part,* and informal or imprecise use of verbs such as *the client felt that*

   a. diffuse meaning and weaken statements.

   b. add warmth to dull scientific prose.

   c. have a place even in serious scientific writing.

   d. can be used to enhance communication.

   e. are more acceptable in written as compared with oral communication.

8. Which of the following should be used in scientific writing?

   a. rhyming

   b. poetic expressions

   c. sexist language

   d. none of the above

9. Edit the following for the use of nonsexist language:

The data in Table 2 are the proportion of male participants who selected the competitive action over the cooperative one on each trial and, similarly, the proportion of female participants who were willing to act aggressively on each trial.

   a. leave as is

   b. The data in Table 2 are the proportion of male and female participants who selected the competitive action over the cooperative one on each trial.

   c. The data in Table 2 are the proportion of male participants who selected the competitive action over the cooperative one on each trial and the proportion of female participants who were willing to act aggressively on each trial.

   d. The data in Table 2 are the proportion of males who selected the competitive action over the cooperative one on each trial and, similarly, the proportion of females who were willing to act in typically male fashion (aggressively) on each trial.

10. In choosing nouns referring to ethnic groups, one should use

   a. the preferred designation within a particular group.

   b. the standard terms of the media.

   c. anthropological terms.

   d. none of the above.

11. Edit the following for verb tense:

Wrightsman (2006) would demonstrate the same effect.

   a. leave as is

   b. Wrightsman (2006) demonstrated the same effect.

   c. Wrightsman (2006) demonstrate the same effect.

   d. The same effect was demonstrated by Wrightsman (2006).

12. Which of the following sentences is grammatically correct?

   a. Name the participant whom you found scored above the median.

   b. The instructions that were included in the experiment were complex.

   c. We had nothing to do with them being the winners.

   d. None of the above is correct.

13. Edit the following for the placement of modifiers:

To manipulate ego-involvement, the respondents were given different average scores for their norm group.

   a. leave as is

   b. To manipulate ego-involvement, we gave the respondents different average scores for their norm group.

   c. Manipulating ego-involvement, the respondents were given different average scores for their norm group.

   d. The respondents were given different average scores for their norm group to manipulate ego-involvement.

14. Edit the following for the use of subordinate conjunctions:

The more skilled athletes chose individual sports, while the less skilled athletes chose team sports.

a. leave as is
b. The more skilled athletes chose individual sports, and, at the same time, the less skilled athletes chose team sports.
c. The more skilled athletes chose individual sports, but the less skilled athletes chose team sports.
d. Both a and b are correct.

15. In most cases, space once after all of the following punctuation marks except

a. periods in a reference citation.
b. internal periods in abbreviations.
c. periods ending a sentence.
d. colons.

16. Edit the following for punctuation:

The confederate always sat to the experimenter's immediate left and the experimenter began the discussion by asking the confederate to evaluate the therapist's degree of empathy.

a. leave as is
b. The confederate always sat to the experimenter's immediate left; and the experimenter began the discussion by asking the confederate to evaluate the therapist's degree of empathy.
c. The confederate always sat to the experimenter's immediate left, the experimenter began the discussion by asking the confederate to evaluate the therapist's degree of empathy.
d. The confederate always sat to the experimenter's immediate left. The experimenter began the discussion by asking the confederate to evaluate the therapist's degree of empathy.

17. Use a semicolon

a. to set off a nonessential or nonrestrictive clause.
b. to separate two independent clauses that are not joined by a conjunction.
c. in references between place of publication and publisher.
d. to do all of the above.

18. Edit the following for the punctuation of ratios:

Moving from the lowest subordinate level of the organization to the highest executive level, the ratios of men to women were 1.2 to 1, 2 to 1, 6 to 1, and 14 to 1, respectively.

a. leave as is
b. Moving from the lowest subordinate level of the organization to the highest executive level, the ratios of men/women were 1.2/1, 2/1, 6/1, and 14/1, respectively.
c. Moving from the lowest subordinate level of the organization to the highest executive level, the ratios of men:women were 1.2:1, 2:1, 6:1, and 14:1, respectively.
d. Moving from the lowest subordinate level of the organization to the highest executive level, the ratios of men-women were 1.2-1, 2-1, 6-1, and 14-1, respectively.

19. Edit the following for punctuation:

The children: none of whom had previously heard the story: listened as a master storyteller told the story.

 a. leave as is
 b. The children; none of whom had previously heard the story; listened as a master storyteller told the story.
 c. The children . . . none of whom had previously heard the story . . . listened as a master storyteller told the story.
 d. The children—none of whom had previously heard the story—listened as a master storyteller told the story.

20. Punctuation is used incorrectly in which example?

 a. The results were significant (see Figure 5).
 b. Walker and Wang, 2009, reported results similar to those of Ho and Card (2001).
 c. Rats that have sustained bilateral excitotoxic lesions of the ventral hippocampus as neonates develop behavioral abnormalities as adults (Powell et al., 2006).
 d. "When sea turtles were studied, the effect was not seen" (p. 276).

21. Edit the following for quotation from a source:

According to Diamond (2008), "the mind and brain often tend to work at a relatively gross level and only with effort (often in the form of inhibition) work more selectively, even in adults" [p. 4].

 a. leave as is
 b. According to Diamond (2008), "the mind and brain often tend to work at a relatively gross level and only with effort (often in the form of inhibition) work more selectively, even in adults" p. 4.
 c. According to Diamond (2008), "the mind and brain often tend to work at a relatively gross level and only with effort (often in the form of inhibition) work more selectively, even in adults (p. 4)."
 d. According to Diamond (2008), "the mind and brain often tend to work at a relatively gross level and only with effort (often in the form of inhibition) work more selectively, even in adults" (p. 4).

22. Which of the following examples needs a hyphen?

 a. a posteriori test
 b. Type II error
 c. 12th grade students
 d. unbiased

23. Which of the examples contains incorrect capitalization?

 a. During Trial 5, Group B performed at criterion.
 b. Column 5, Row 3
 c. The animals ate Purina Lab Chow after tail-pinch administration.
 d. In his book, *History of Psychology,* the author describes Small's first use of the white rat.

24. Edit the following for the format for anchor points on a rating scale:

    The respondents ranked each of the 30 characteristics on a scale ranging from "most like my mother" (1) to "most like my father" (5).

    a. leave as is
    b. The respondents ranked each of the 30 characteristics on a scale ranging from MOST LIKE MY MOTHER (1) to MOST LIKE MY FATHER (5).
    c. The respondents ranked each of the 30 characteristics on a scale ranging from: most like my mother (1) to: most like my father (5).
    d. The respondents ranked each of the 30 characteristics on a scale ranging from 1 (*most like my mother*) to 5 (*most like my father*).

25. Which word in the following sentence should be italicized?

    Snails were much faster when allowed to bathe ad lib in the acetylcholine solution.

    a. acetylcholine
    b. ad lib
    c. snails
    d. bathe
    e. none of the above

26. Which Latin abbreviation is used incorrectly in the following example?

    When management styles were compared (authoritarian vs. participatory), it was found that authoritarian managers, i.e., those who did not solicit or act on input from subordinates, did not do well in smaller organizations (e.g., corporations with fewer than 100 employees).

    a. vs.
    b. i.e.
    c. e.g.
    d. all of the above
    e. none of the above

27. Direct quotations

    a. must follow the wording, spelling, and interior punctuation of the original source even if incorrect. Errors in the original source are indicated with [*sic*].
    b. must follow the wording and interior punctuation of the original source, but any spelling errors should be corrected.
    c. should follow the original source but minor changes in wording, spelling, and interior punctuation are permissible.
    d. None of the above is correct.

28. When citing a direct quotation from a source, be sure to give

    a. the authors' names.
    b. the year of publication.
    c. the page number or other locator, such as paragraph number.
    d. all of the above.
    e. the authors' names and the year of publication.

29. Edit the following for the citation of a reference in text:

    The acquisition of knowledge about human behavior and the development and continued use of relational skills have the potential to enhance functioning in personal and family lives (e.g., Guy, 1987; Norcross & Aboyoun, 1994).

    a. leave as is
    b. The acquisition of knowledge about human behavior and the development and continued use of relational skills have the potential to enhance functioning in personal and family lives (e.g., Norcross & Aboyoun, 1994; Guy, 1987).
    c. The acquisition of knowledge about human behavior and the development and continued use of relational skills have the potential to enhance functioning in personal and family lives (e.g., Guy, 1987, Norcross & Aboyoun, 1994).
    d. The acquisition of knowledge about human behavior and the development and continued use of relational skills have the potential to enhance functioning in personal and family lives (e.g., Guy: 1987; Norcross & Aboyoun: 1994).

30. Edit the following for the citation of a reference in text:

    In three studies with college students, self-esteem was not longitudinally related to depression (Butler, A. C., et al., 1994; Lakey, B, 1988; Roberts, J. E., & Gotlib, I. H., 1997), and in a study of adolescents, self-esteem at age 14 did not predict depression at age 18 (Block, J. H., Gjerde, P. F., & Block, J. H., 1991).

    a. leave as is
    b. In three studies with college students, self-esteem was not longitudinally related to depression (Butler et al., 1994; Lakey, 1988; J. E. Roberts & Gotlib, 1997), and in a study of adolescents, self-esteem at age 14 did not predict depression at age 18 (Block, Gjerde, & Block, 1991).
    c. In three studies with college students, self-esteem was not longitudinally related to depression (Butler et al., 1994; Lakey, 1988; J. E. Roberts and Gotlib, 1997), and in a study of adolescents, self-esteem at age 14 did not predict depression at age 18 (Block, Gjerde, and Block, 1991)
    d. In three studies with college students, self-esteem was not longitudinally related to depression (J. E. Roberts & Gotlib, 1997, Butler et al., 1994, Lakey, 1988;), and in a study of adolescents, self-esteem at age 14 did not predict depression at age 18 (Block, Gjerde, & Block, 1991).

31. Choose the correct citation:

    a. (Birman et al., 2005; Espin, 2006; Falicov, 1998; Hondagneu-Sotelo & Avila, 1997; Perez Foster, 2001)
    b. (Greenleaf, 1977/2002).
    c. (Hondagneu-Sotelo & Avila, 1997; Falicov, 1998)
    d. b and c
    e. a and b

32. Edit the following for the citation of references in text:

    As humans we have an emotional need to experience "belongingness" or "relatedness" (Baumeister & Leary, 1995; see also Reis & Collins, 2000; Burleson, Albrecht, & Sarason, 1994).

    a. leave as is
    b. As humans we have an emotional need to experience "belongingness" or "relatedness" (Baumeister & Leary, 1995; see also Burleson, Albrecht, & Sarason, 1994; Reis & Collins, 2000).
    c. As humans we have an emotional need to experience "belongingness" or "relatedness" (Baumeister and Leary, 1995; see also Burleson, Albrecht, and Sarason, 1994; Reis and Collins, 2000).
    d. As humans we have an emotional need to experience "belongingness" or "relatedness" (Baumeister & Leary, 1995, see also Burleson, Albrecht, & Sarason, 1994, Reis & Collins, 2000).

33. If no author is given for a source, put the source in the correct order in the reference list by

    a. moving the title to the author position and alphabetizing by the first significant word of the title.
    b. beginning the entry with the word *Anonymous* and alphabetizing as if this were the author's name.
    c. moving the journal title or publishing house to the author position and alphabetizing by the first significant word of the name.
    d. Doing none of the above.

34. In a reference list, when ordering several works by the same first author,

    a. place single-author entries before multiple-author entries.
    b. write "ibid." for the first author's name after the first entry.
    c. order them alphabetically by the name of the journal.
    d. do all of the above.

35. Edit the following for the application of APA reference style:

Herbst-Damm, K. L., & Kulik, J. A. (2005). Volunteer support, marital status, and the survival times of terminally ill patients. *Health Psychology, 24,* 225–229. DOI.10.1037/0278-6133.24.2.225

a. Leave as is
b. Herbst-Damm, K. L., & Kulik, J. A. (2005). Volunteer support, marital status, and the survival times of terminally ill patients. *Health Psychology, 24,* 225–229. doi:10.1037/0278-6133.24.2.225
c. Herbst-Damm, K. L., & Kulik, J. A. (2005). Volunteer support, marital status, and the survival times of terminally ill patients. *Health Psychology, 24,* 225–229. 10.1037/0278-6133.24.2.225
d. Herbst-Damm, K. L., & Kulik, J. A. (2005). Volunteer support, marital status, and the survival times of terminally ill patients. *Health Psychology, 24,* 225–229. [doi:10.1037/0278-6133.24.2.225]

36. Edit the following for the application of APA reference style:

Laplace, P.-S. (1951/1814). *A philosophical essay on probabilities* (F. W. Truscott & F. L. Emory, Trans.). New York, NY: Dover. (Original work published 1814)

a. leave as is
b. Laplace, P.-S. (1951). *A philosophical essay on probabilities* (F. W. Truscott & F. L. Emory, Trans.). (Original work published 1814). New York, NY: Dover.
c. Laplace, P.-S. (1951). *A philosophical essay on probabilities* (F. W. Truscott & F. L. Emory, Trans.). New York, NY: Dover. (Original work published 1814)
d. Laplace, P.-S. (1951). [*A philosophical essay on probabilities*] (F. W. Truscott & F. L. Emory, Translators.). New York, NY: Dover. (Original work published 1814)

37. Edit the following for the application of APA reference style:

Katz, I., Gabayan, K., & Aghajan, H. (2007). A Multi-Touch Surface Using Multiple Cameras. In J. Blanc-Talon, W. Philips, D. Popescu, & P. Scheunders (Eds.), *Lecture Notes in Computer Science: Vol. 4678. Advanced Concepts for Intelligent Vision Systems* (pp. 97–108). Berlin, Germany: Springer-Verlag. doi:10.1007/978-3-540-74607-2_9

a. leave as is
b. Katz, I., Gabayan, K., & Aghajan, H. (2007). A multi-touch surface using multiple cameras. In J. Blanc-Talon, W. Philips, D. Popescu, & P. Scheunders (Eds.), *Lecture Notes in Computer Science: Vol. 4678. Advanced Concepts for Intelligent Vision Systems* (pp. 97–108). Berlin, Germany: Springer-Verlag. doi:10.1007/978-3-540-74607-2_9
c. Katz, Gabayan, & Aghajan. (2007). A multi-touch surface using multiple cameras. In Blanc-Talon, Philips, Popescu, & Scheunders (Eds.), *Lecture Notes in Computer Science: Vol. 4678. Advanced Concepts for Intelligent Vision Systems* (pp. 97–108). Berlin, Germany: Springer-Verlag. doi:10.1007/978-3-540-74607-2_9
d. Katz, I., Gabayan, K., & Aghajan, H. (2007, December). A multi-touch surface using multiple cameras. In J. Blanc-Talon, W. Philips, D. Popescu, & P. Scheunders (Eds.), *Lecture Notes in Computer Science: Vol. 4678. Advanced Concepts for Intelligent Vision Systems*. Berlin, Germany: Springer-Verlag. doi:10.1007/978-3-540-74607-2_9

38. Edit the following for the application of APA reference style:

    Van Nuys, D. (Producer). (2007, December 19). *Shrink rap radio* [Audio podcast]. Retrieved from
        http://www.shrinkrapradio.com/

    a. leave as is
    b. Van Nuys, D. (2007, December 19). *Shrink rap radio* [Audio podcast]. Retrieved from http://
        www.shrinkrapradio.com/
    c. Van Nuys, D. (Producer). (2007, December 19). *Shrink rap radio.* Audio podcast. Retrieved from
        http://www.shrinkrapradio.com/
    d. Van Nuys, D. (Producer). (December 19). *Shrink rap radio* [Audio podcast]. Retrieved from
        http://www.shrinkrapradio.com/

39. A digital object identifier is generally located

    a. on the first page of the electronic or print version of an article, near the copyright notice.
    b. in a footnote on the first page of an electronic or print version of an article.
    c. on the database landing page for the article.
    d. all of the above.
    e. a and c.

40. Which kind of spacing should not be used anywhere in a manuscript?

    a. single-spacing
    b. double-spacing
    c. triple-spacing
    d. all of the above

41. The right margin should

    a. have divided words to achieve an even margin.
    b. not have divided words and may be uneven.
    c. have a 1-in. (2.54-cm) space rather than a 2-in. (5.08-cm) space.
    d. have divided or undivided words to achieve a clean line.

42. The correct order of manuscript pages is

    a. abstract, text, tables, figures, references, appendices
    b. text, references, tables, figures, abstract, appendices
    c. abstract, text, references, tables, figures, appendices
    d. abstract, text, appendices, references, tables, figures

43. Edit the following for typing a title page:

THE SLEEPER EFFECT IN PERSUASION:

A META-ANALYTIC REVIEW

G. Tarcan Kumkale and Dolores Albarracín

University of Florida

a. leave as is

b.

The Sleeper Effect in Persuasion:

A Meta-Analytic Review

G. Tarcan Kumkale and Dolores Albarracín

University of Florida

c.

The Sleeper Effect in Persuasion:

A Meta-Analytic Review

G. Tarcan Kumkale & Dolores Albarracín

University of Florida

d.

The Sleeper Effect in Persuasion:

A Meta-Analytic Review

G. Tarcan Kumkale   Dolores Albarracín

University of Florida   University of Florida

TERM PAPER PRACTICE TEST
ANSWER SHEET AND FEEDBACK REPORT

Student Name _____ Date _____

Question Number	Answer	APA Codes	Question Number	Answer	APA Codes
1	_____	2.01–2.05	22	_____	4.12–4.13
2	_____	3.01–3.03	23	_____	4.14–4.20
3	_____	3.01–3.04	24	_____	4.21
4	_____	3.04	25	_____	4.21
5	_____	3.05–3.06	26	_____	4.22–4.30
6	_____	3.08–3.09	27	_____	6.03–6.10
7	_____	3.08–3.09	28	_____	6.03–6.10
8	_____	3.08–3.11	29	_____	6.11–6.21
9	_____	3.12–3.17	30	_____	6.11–6.21
10	_____	3.12–3.17	31	_____	6.11–6.21
11	_____	3.18–3.19	32	_____	6.11–6.21
12	_____	3.20–3.23	33	_____	6.22–6.25
13	_____	3.20–3.23	34	_____	6.22–6.25
14	_____	3.20–3.23	35	_____	6.27–6.31, 7.01
15	_____	4.01–4.11	36	_____	6.27–6.31, 7.02
16	_____	4.01–4.11	37	_____	6.27–6.31, 7.04
17	_____	4.01–4.11	38	_____	6.27–6.31, 7.07
18	_____	4.01–4.11	39	_____	6.31
19	_____	4.01–4.11	40	_____	8.03
20	_____	4.01–4.11	41	_____	8.03
21	_____	4.01–4.11	42	_____	8.03
			43	_____	8.03

NUMBER CORRECT _____

TERM PAPER PRACTICE TEST
ANSWER KEY

Question Number	Answer	APA Codes	Question Number	Answer	APA Codes
1	c	2.01–2.05	22	c	4.12–4.13
2	d	3.01–3.03	23	b	4.14–4.20
3	d	3.01–3.04	24	d	4.21
4	d	3.04	25	e	4.21
5	e	3.05–3.06	26	b	4.22–4.30
6	d	3.08–3.09	27	a	6.03–6.10
7	d	3.08–3.09	28	d	6.03–6.10
8	d	3.08–3.11	29	a	6.11–6.21
9	b	3.12–3.17	30	b	6.11–6.21
10	b	3.12–3.17	31	e	6.11–6.21
11	b	3.18–3.19	32	b	6.11–6.21
12	b	3.20–3.23	33	a	6.22–6.25
13	b	3.20–3.23	34	a	6.22–6.25
14	a	3.20–3.23	35	b	6.27–6.31, 7.01
15	c	4.01–4.11	36	c	6.27–6.31, 7.02
16	d	4.01–4.11	37	b	6.27–6.31, 7.04
17	b	4.01–4.11	38	a	6.27–6.31, 7.07
18	c	4.01–4.11	39	e	6.31
19	d	4.01–4.11	40	c	8.03
20	b	4.01–4.11	41	c	8.03
21	d	4.01–4.11	42	a	8.03
			43	b	8.03

Term Paper Review Exercises

NOTES:

Review Exercise: Parts of a Manuscript

Running head: COMMUNICATION MODELS OF ORGANIZATIONS

Computer Simulations of Communication Processes in Vertically

Structured Organizations

Hy R. Kichal, Art E. Fishel, and Mack N. Tosh

Upsy Downsy National University

Millie Tarry and B. Yuri Craddick

Department of Political Chemistry

Unelectoral College

1

APA CODES: 2.01–2.13, 8.03

Term Paper Review Exercises

Review exercises are all in the integrative format and cover the same style rules as the learning exercises and integrative exercises. Complete the review exercises as you did the integrative exercises, by reading the exercises on the right-hand page, writing your corrections on that page, and comparing your corrections with the correct version of the exercise on the left. Review exercises are designed to give you additional practice, to help you review style points you have already studied, and to further prepare you to take a mastery test.

Review Exercise: Parts of a Manuscript

Computer simulations of communication processes in vertically

structured organizations

Hy R. Kichal, Art E. Fishel, Mack N. Tosh

Upsy Downsy National University

Millie Tarry & B. Yuri Craddick

Department of Political Chemistry, Unelectoral College

Communication Models of Organizations

APA CODES: 2.01–2.13, 8.03

Review Exercise: Headings and Series

A History of Psychology

Early Laboratories

Harvard laboratories.

James's basement. Because Harvard University would not allow live animals on campus, William James converted the basement of his home into an animal laboratory. Edward Lee Thorndike did some of his first research on chickens in James's basement.

APA CODES: 3.02–3.03

Review Exercise: Guidelines to Reduce Bias in Language

In North America, the term *minority* may apply to ethnic, religious, national, and sexual minorities; elders; people who are poor, less formally educated, or of rural or Indigenous heritage; people who have a disability; and women and children. All of these populations fit the definition of culture as broadly defined, and all have traditionally been excluded, marginalized, or misrepresented by mainstream psychology; in this sense, they may be considered cultural minorities. (European American children and adolescents are somewhat of an exception, in that although they may be considered minorities in relation to the larger society, they have been the focus of much attention in psychology, beginning with Freud's developmental interests; this is not true for children and adolescents of ethnic minority cultures.)

But there is more to being a member of a minority culture than the experience of oppression. Identification with a minority culture or group may also lead to the development of positive traits and qualities that may not develop in people whose lives are buffered by privilege (McIntosh, 1998, p. 101).

Minority status may bring with it unique forms of knowledge, awareness, emotional and tangible support, a sense of community, and an opportunity to contribute to others in ways that are deeply meaningful (Newman & Newman, 1999). A therapist needs to be aware that describing a group of people as a minority culture is different from referring to a person as a minority. The latter may be perceived as disempowering because it places a label on the individual as well as an entire group.

APA CODES: 3.12–3.17, 4.21

Review Exercise: Headings and Series

A History of Psychology

Early Laboratories

Harvard Laboratories:

James's Basement: Because Harvard University would not allow live animals on campus, William James converted the basement of his home into an animal laboratory. Edward Lee Thorndike did some of his first research on chickens in James's basement.

APA CODES: 3.02–3.03

Review Exercise: Guidelines to Reduce Bias in Language

In North America, the term minority may apply to ethnic, religious, national, and sexual minorities; the elderly; the uneducated, or those of rural or Indigenous heritage; the disabled; and females and children. All of these populations fit the definition of culture as broadly defined, and all have traditionally been excluded, marginalized, or misrepresented by mainstream psychology; in this sense, they may be considered cultural minorities. (European American children and adolescents are somewhat of an exception, in that although they may be considered minorities in relation to the larger society, they have been the focus of much attention in psychology, beginning with Freud's developmental interests; this is not true for children and adolescents of ethnic minority cultures.)

But there is more to being a member of a minority culture than the experience of oppression. Identification with a minority culture or group may also lead some men to develop positive traits and qualities that may not develop in other men whose lives are buffered by privilege (McIntosh, 1998, p. 101). A man's minority status may bring with it unique forms of knowledge, awareness, emotional and tangible support, a sense of community, and an opportunity to contribute to others in ways that are deeply meaningful (Newman & Newman, 1999). A therapist needs to be aware that describing a group of people as a minority culture is different from his referring to a person as a minority. The latter may be perceived as disempowering because it places a label on the man as well as an entire group.

APA CODES: 3.12–3.17, 4.21

Review Exercise: Grammar

Research from the expectancy-value perspective has examined the values that individuals perceive when engaging in tasks and how these task values are related to subsequent achievement choices. Eccles and her colleagues (Eccles et al., 1983; see Eccles, 2005, for a review) have identified several types of task value that are important in predicting motivation and achievement, in addition to the well-documented effects of success expectancies (Bandura, 1997; Pintrich & Schunk, 2002). Two of these task values are *utility* and *intrinsic* value. Tasks with utility value are important because they are useful and relevant beyond the immediate situation for other tasks or aspects of a person's life. Tasks with intrinsic value are important to the individual because they are enjoyable and fun. Individuals can discover and appreciate the value of activities through interaction and experience. Perceiving utility and/or intrinsic value in tasks has been associated with motivation and interest in activities. For example, both intrinsic and utility value have been found to predict motivational outcomes such as course enrollment decisions (Harackiewicz, Durik, Barron, Linnenbrink-Garcia, & Tauer, 2008; Meece, Wigfield, & Eccles, 1990; Updegraff, Eccles, Barber, & O'Brien, 1996; Wigfield, 1994), self-reported effort in science classes (Cole, Bergin, & Whittaker, 2006; Mac Iver, Stipek, & Daniels, 1991), intentions to continue a school-based running program (Xiang, Chen, & Bruene, 2005), amount of free time spent on sports (Eccles & Harold, 1991), and classroom interest (Durik, 2003).

Whereas both intrinsic and utility task values have been linked to motivation, utility value may be uniquely related to achievement. For example, Simons, Dewitte, and Lens (2003) found that highlighting the usefulness of an activity—by telling participants how it could help them achieve their future goals—increased persistence and performance in a physical education class. Bong (2001b) found that the perceived usefulness of a course predicted self-efficacy in the course, which in turn predicted exam performance. Malka and Covington (2005) found that the relevance of school work to students' future goals (i.e., perceived instrumentality) predicted classroom performance. These studies indicate that there is a relationship between perceiving utility in a task and subsequent performance.

APA CODES: 3.18–3.23, 4.03, 4.21

Review Exercise: Grammar

Research from the expectancy-value perspective has been examining the values which individuals perceive when engaging in tasks, and how these task values are related to subsequent achievement choices. Eccles and her colleagues (Eccles et al., 1983; see Eccles, 2005, for a review) identify several types of task value that are important in predicting motivation and achievement, in addition to the well-documented effects of success expectancies (Bandura, 1997; Pintrich & Schunk, 2002). Two of these task values are utility and intrinsic value. Tasks with utility value are important since they are useful and relevant beyond the immediate situation, for other tasks or aspects of a person's life. Tasks with intrinsic value are important to the individual because they are enjoyable and fun. Individuals can discover and appreciate the value of activities through interaction and experience. Perceiving utility and/or intrinsic value in tasks has been associated with motivation and interest in activities. For example, both intrinsic and utility value have found to predict motivational outcomes such as course enrollment decisions (Harackiewicz, Durik, Barron, Linnenbrink-Garcia, & Tauer, 2008; Meece, Wigfield, & Eccles, 1990; Updegraff, Eccles, Barber, & O'Brien, 1996; Wigfield, 1994), self-reported effort in science classes (Cole, Bergin, & Whittaker, 2006; Mac Iver, Stipek, & Daniels, 1991), intentions to continue a school-based running program (Xiang, Chen, & Bruene, 2005), amount of free time spent on sports (Eccles & Harold, 1991), and classroom interest (Durik, 2003).

While both intrinsic and utility task values have been linked to motivation, utility value may be uniquely related to achievement. For example, Simons, Dewitte, and Lens (2003) find that highlighting the usefulness of an activity—by telling participants how it could help him or her achieve his or her future goals—increased persistence and performance in a physical education class. Bong (2001b) finds that the perceived usefulness of a course predicted self-efficacy in the course, that in turn predicted exam performance. Malka and Covington (2005) find that the relevance of school work to students' future goals (i.e., perceived instrumentality) predicted classroom performance. These studies have indicated that there is a relationship between perceiving utility in a task and subsequent performance.

APA CODES: 3.18–3.23, 4.03, 4.21

Review Exercise: Punctuation

Cardiovascular disease is subject to a number of risk factors. Some of the risk factors—family history of heart disease, age, and gender—are genetic or cannot be modified but are important to identify for the purpose of monitoring cardiac functioning. Other risk factors—cholesterol levels, cigarette smoking, and hypertension—can be modified and therefore pose opportunities for the prevention of coronary disease or heart attacks. Cholesterol levels can be reduced through dietary modifications; cigarette smoking requires an obvious behavioral change; and hypertension, although often treated pharmacologically, can also be treated behaviorally. Given the potential side effects of antihypertension drugs and the frequent failures to take medications (perhaps resulting from the absence of overt symptoms), behavioral treatments are an attractive alternative or supplement to medical treatments. Hypertension can be reduced through dietary changes (resulting in weight reduction and diminished salt intake), increased exercise, and improvement in stress-coping skills. More direct effects on blood pressure are achieved through biofeedback and relaxation training.

APA CODES: 4.01–4.11

Review Exercise: Spelling and Hyphenation

Forgiveness of blasphemy was explored in a 2 × 2 between-subjects factorial design. Low-dogmatic individuals were compared with high-dogmatic individuals in their willingness to forgive a person who published a blasphemous essay or a highly revealing, kiss-and-tell essay. Blood pressure readings were taken before and after the forgiveness ratings. Planned comparisons were reported rather than the results of a two-way analysis of variance. Individuals who were high dogmatic were significantly less forgiving than low-dogmatic individuals, as determined by planned *t* tests. Blood pressure was highest in the lowest forgiveness condition.

APA CODES: 4.12–4.13

Review Exercise: Punctuation

Cardiovascular disease is subject to a number of risk factors. Some of the risk factors; family history of heart disease, age, gender, are genetic or cannot be modified, but are important to identify for the purpose of monitoring cardiac functioning, and other risk factors: cholesterol levels, cigarette smoking, hypertension, can be modified, and therefore pose opportunities for the prevention of coronary disease or heart attacks. Cholesterol levels can be reduced through dietary modifications, cigarette smoking requires an obvious behavioral change, and hypertension (although often treated pharmacologically) can also be treated behaviorally. Given the potential side effects of antihypertension drugs and the frequent failures to take medications (Perhaps resulting from the absence of overt symptoms.), behavioral treatments are an attractive alternative or supplement to medical treatments. Hypertension can be reduced through dietary changes (resulting in weight reduction, and diminished salt intake), increased exercise and improvement in stress-coping skills. More direct effects on blood pressure are achieved through biofeedback, and relaxation training.

APA CODES: 4.01–4.11

Review Exercise: Spelling and Hyphenation

Forgivness of blasfemy was explored in a 2 × 2 between-subjects factorial design. Low dogmatic individuals were compared with high dogmatic individuals in their willingness to forgive a person who published a blasfemous essay or a highly-revealing, kiss and tell essay. Blood-pressure readings were taken before-and-after the forgiveness-ratings. Planned compairsons were reported rather than the results of a two way analysis-of-variance. Individuals who were high-dogmatic were significantly less forgiving than low dogmatic individauls, as determined by planned *t*-tests. Blood-pressure was highest in the lowest-forgiveness condition.

APA CODES: 4.12–4.13

Review Exercise: Capitalization

Not all explanations of spider phobia assume that classical conditioning of irrational fear occurred at some point in the life of a patient (e.g., neo-Freudian theories). In fact, some theories of learning contend that there are biological constraints that favor the acquisition of some phobias over others (e.g., the biological preparedness theories of Garcia & Koelling, 1966, or Maser & Seligman, 1977).

APA CODES: 4.14–4.20

Review Exercise: Italics

Ranking scores range from 1 (*best*) to 25 (*worst*), with lower numbers representing more positive evaluations. Rankings were calculated for each participant by assigning a rank of 1 to the item with the highest rating, a rank of 2 to the next highest rating, and so on. The mean rank score was used to resolve ties when multiple items received the same rating. Rankings were compared across groups using the nonparametric Mann–Whitney *U* test. Self-reported quality of life was compared across groups and compared with scenario ratings, using independent samples *t* tests.

APA CODE: 4.21

Review Exercise: Abbreviations

The Levels of Attributional Change Scale (LAC; Bellis, 1993) is a self-report measure; participants are asked to rate 33 statements about the cause of their procrastination on a 7-point Likert-type scale from 1 (*strongly disagree*) to 7 (*strongly agree*). The LAC provides scores on 10 subscales, each indicative of a particular etiological locus for attributions (environment, interpersonal conflicts, intrapersonal conflicts, family of origin, biology, bad luck, insufficient effort, fate, maladaptive thoughts, and deliberate lifestyle choices). LAC items are empirically derived from people's spontaneous attributions (e.g., Norcross, Prochaska, Guadagnoli, & DiClemente, 1984), and 10 separate (but correlated) factors have been confirmed for this scale through factor analyses on three separate samples (Bellis, 1993; Norcross et al., 1984). For this study, an 11th theoretically relevant factor—lack of needed skills—was added in the form of two items ("a lack of study skills" and "the fact that I never learned skills needed for my courses"). Some items were also reworded slightly to increase their relevance to procrastination. Exploratory factor analysis did not suggest that these changes substantially altered the LAC's factor structure. Retest reliability for the LAC averages .70 at a 4-week interval (Bellis, 1993), and the LAC's discriminant validity is supported by its low correlation with the Attributional Style Questionnaire, a measure of causal dimensions (Norcross & Magaletta, 1990), and with the Causal Dimension Scale in the current sample.

APA CODES: 4.22–4.30

Review Exercise: Capitalization

Not all explanations of Spider Phobia assume that classical conditioning of irrational fear occurred at some point in the life of a patient (e.g., Neo-Freudian theories), in fact, some theories of learning contend that there are biological constraints that favor the acquisition of some phobias over others (e.g., the Biological Preparedness theories of Garcia & Koelling, 1966, or Maser & Seligman, 1977).

APA CODES: 4.14–4.20

Review Exercise: Italics

Ranking scores range from 1 ("best") to 25 ("worst"), with lower numbers representing *more positive* evaluations. Rankings were calculated for each participant by assigning a rank of 1 to the item with the highest rating, a rank of 2 to the next highest rating, and so on. The *mean* rank score was used to resolve ties when multiple items received the same rating. Rankings were compared across groups using the nonparametric Mann–Whitney U test. Self-reported quality of life was compared across groups, and compared with scenario ratings, using independent samples t tests.

APA CODE: 4.21

Review Exercise: Abbreviations

The LAC (Bellis, 1993) is a self-report measure; participants are asked to rate 33 statements about the cause of their procrastination on a 7-pt Likert-type scale from 1 (*strongly disagree*) to 7 (*strongly agree*). The LAC provides scores on 10 subscales, each indicative of a particular etiological locus for attributions (environment, interpersonal conflicts, intrapersonal conflicts, family of origin, biology, bad luck, insufficient effort, fate, maladaptive thoughts, and deliberate lifestyle choices). LAC items are empirically derived from people's spontaneous attributions (for example, Norcross, Prochaska, Guadagnoli, & DiClemente, 1984), and 10 separate (but correlated) factors have been confirmed for this scale through factor analyses on three separate samples (Bellis, 1993; Norcross et al., 1984). For this study, an 11th theoretically relevant factor—lack of needed skills—was added in the form of two items ("a lack of study skills" and "the fact that I never learned skills needed for my courses"). Some items were also reworded slightly to increase their relevance to procrastination. EFA did not suggest that these changes substantially altered the LAC's factor structure. Retest reliability for the LAC averages .70 at a 4-wk interval (Bellis, 1993), and the LAC's discriminant validity is supported by its low correlation with the ASQ, a measure of causal dimensions (Norcross & Magaletta, 1990), and with the Causal Dimension Scale in the current sample.

APA CODES: 4.22–4.30

Review Exercise: Quotations

According to Kurtz (1988), near death experiences (NDEs) have reasonable physiological explanations: "We know that when the body is badly injured the heart stops and cerebral anoxia occurs. . . . At first there may be a sense of well-being, probably the result of the brain's endorphin response to extreme trauma" (p. 15).

APA CODES: 4.08, 6.03–6.09

Review Exercise: Reference Citations in Text

In any one year, an estimated 250 in 100,000 children in the United States experience traumatic brain injury (TBI; Anderson, Northam, Hendy, & Wrennall, 2001). As many as 15% of individuals with mild TBI continue to have significant problems after the injury (Hibbard, Gordon, Martin, Raskin, & Brown, 2001). The effects of TBI can range from minimal to significant and can become immediately evident or emerge after a significant delay (Eslinger & Biddle, 2000).

A considerable body of literature documents a high likelihood of personality changes following a moderate to severe TBI (Golden & Golden, 2003; McGee, 2004). Disorders of behavior and personality may emerge, including agitation, depression, attention deficits, problems with executive functioning, and lack of self-control (McGee, 2004). Viguier, Dellatolas, Gasquet, Martin, and Choquet (2001) found that school delay and school problems, depression, psychological difficulties, aggressive behavior, and disturbed social interactions were significantly more prevalent in a TBI group compared with a control group.

Therapeutic interventions for TBI include insight-oriented psychotherapy, cognitive–behavioral and behavioral therapy, relaxation training, social skills therapy, and anger management techniques (Beatty, 2004). As noted by Hibbard et al. (2001), outcomes vary considerably for children who endure TBI, with no two cases alike.

APA CODES: 6.11–6.21

Review Exercise: Quotations

According to Kurtz (1988, p. 15), near death experiences (NDEs) have reasonable physiological explanations:

> We know that when the body is badly injured the heart stops and cerebral anoxia occurs . . . At first there may be a sense of well-being, probably the result of the brain's endorphin response to extreme trauma.

APA CODES: 4.08, 6.03–6.09

Review Exercise: Reference Citations in Text

In any one year, an estimated 250 in 100,000 children in the United States experience traumatic brain injury (TBI; Anderson, Northam, Hendy, Wrennall, 2001). As many as 15% of individuals with mild TBI continue to have significant problems after the injury (Hibbard, et al., 2001). The effects of TBI can range from minimal to significant and can become immediately evident or emerge after a significant delay (Eslinger & Biddle, 2000).

A considerable body of literature documents a high likelihood of personality changes following a moderate to severe TBI (McGee, 2004; Golden and Golden, 2003;). Disorders of behavior and personality may emerge, including agitation, depression, attention deficits, problems with executive functioning, and lack of self-control (2004). Viguier, Dellatolas, Gasquet, Martin, and Choquet, 2001, found that school delay and school problems, depression, psychological difficulties, aggressive behavior, and disturbed social interactions were significantly more prevalent in a TBI group compared with a control group.

Therapeutic interventions for TBI include insight-oriented psychotherapy, cognitive–behavioral and behavioral therapy, relaxation training, social skills therapy, and anger management techniques (Beatty, 2004). As noted by Hibbard, Gordon, Martin, Raskin, & Brown (2001), outcomes vary considerably for children who endure TBI, with no two cases alike.

APA CODES: 6.11–6.21

Review Exercise: Reference List

References

DeLeon, P. H., Hagglund, K. J., Ragusea, S. A., & Sammons, M. T. (2003). Expanding roles for psychologists: The 21st century. In G. Strieker & T. A. Widiger (Eds.), *Clinical psychology* (Vol. 8, pp. 551–568). New York, NY: Wiley.

DeLeon, P. H., Rossomando, N. P., & Smedley, B. D. (2004). The future is primary care. In R. G. Frank, S. H. McDainiel, J. H. Bray, & M. Heldring (Eds.), *Primary care psychology* (pp. 317–325). Washington, DC: American Psychological Association. doi: 10.1037/10651-017

DeLeon, P. H., & Zimbardo, P. G. (in press). Presidential reflections—Past and future. *American Psychologist.*

Greenberg, D. S. (1999, March 22). Hardly an ounce for prevention. *The Washington Post,* p. 19A.

Greene, J. (2001, January 1). AMA backs limits on scope of nonphysician practice. *American Medical News.* Retrieved from http://www.ama.assn.org/amednews/2001/01/01/prsb0101.htm

Institute of Medicine. (1999). Errors in healthcare. In L. T. Kohn, J. M. Corrigan, & M. S. Donaldson (Eds.), *To err is human: Building a safer health system* (pp. 26–48). Washington, DC: National Academies Press.

U.S. Department of Health and Human Services. (2000). *Healthy people 2010: Understanding and improving health.* Washington, DC: Government Printing Office.

■ *Note to students:* You also should have changed the order of the references because they were not alphabetized correctly.

APA CODES: 6.27–6.32, 7.01–7.11, Appendix 7.1

Review Exercise: Reference List

References

DeLeon, P. H., Hagglund, K. J., Ragusea, S. A., & Sammons, M. T. (2003). Expanding roles for psychologists: The 21st century. In G. Strieker & T. A. Widiger (Eds.), *Clinical psychology, 8,* 551–568. New York, NY: John Wiley & Sons.

DeLeon, P. H., & Zimbardo, P. G. (in press). "Presidential reflections—Past and future." *American Psychologist.*

DeLeon, P. H., Rossomando, N. P., & Smedley, B. D. (2004). The future is primary care. In R. G. Frank, S. H. McDaniel, J. H. Bray, & M. Heldring (Eds.), *Primary Care Psychology* (pp. 317–325). Washington, DC: American Psychological Association. Retrieved from doi:10.1037/10651-017

Greenberg, Daniel S. (1999, March 22). Hardly an ounce for prevention. *The Washington Post,* 19A. Downloaded from http://pqasb.pqarchiver.com/washingtonpost/access/39924181.html?dids=39924 181:39924181&FMT=ABS&FMTS=ABS:FT&date=Mar+22%2C+1999&author=Daniel+S.+Greenberg &pub=The+Washington+Post&edition=&startpage=A.19&desc=Hardly+an+Ounce+for+Prevention

Greene, J. (2001). "AMA backs limits on scope of nonphysician practice." *American Medical News,* January 1.[Electronic version retrieved from http://www.ama.-assn.org/amednews/2001/01/01/ prsb0101.htm]

HHS, U.S. Dept. of. (2000). *Healthy people 2010: Understanding and improving health.* Washington, DC: GPO.

IOM (Institute of Medicine). (1999). Errors in healthcare. In L. T. Kohn, J. M. Corrigan, & M. S. Donaldson (Eds.), *To err is human: Building a safer health system.* Washington, DC: Natl. Acad. Press.

APA CODES: 6.27–6.32, 7.01–7.11, Appendix 7.1

Term Paper Mastery Tests

The *Instructor's Resource Guide* contains four mastery tests for each unit (term paper and research report). Your instructor will decide whether to give you one or more mastery tests as a means to evaluate your knowledge of APA Style and your readiness to prepare writing assignments. These tests are similar in structure and content to the familiarization and practice tests but contain different questions. Your instructor will provide you with the mastery tests and may or may not grade them; a grade is useful only for demonstrating that you have mastered APA Style (90% correct is the standard for mastery unless your instructor announces otherwise).

Like the familiarization and practice tests, the mastery tests contain approximately 40 multiple-choice questions, along with the APA codes indicating where in the *Publication Manual* you can find the answers. However, you may not use the *Publication Manual* while you take the tests. Your instructor will give you either a grade or feedback about the areas in which you need to work.

4

Research Report Unit

The purpose of this unit is to provide you with the chance to learn and apply the APA Style rules that will be most useful when you write research reports. Because this unit contains style requirements that are more advanced or more technical than the exercises in the term paper unit, you should do the latter unit first. This unit, like the term paper unit, is divided into four components: the familiarization test, learning exercises and integrative exercises, the practice test, and review exercises. Begin by taking the familiarization test, which will help you to identify what you do and do not know about APA Style with regard to writing research reports.

Research Report Familiarization Test

By taking this test and reviewing your responses, you will be able to determine whether you are familiar with the APA Style requirements related to writing research reports. The test contains 41 multiple-choice items. There are two answer sheets at the end of the test, one with blanks for you to write in your answers and the other containing the answers. APA codes are next to each answer blank; they correspond to the sections in the *Publication Manual* containing the relevant style rules. Read each test item and the possible responses, and write the letter of the response on the blank answer sheet. You may consult the *Publication Manual* at any time. It may be useful to mark questions that you found to be difficult. After taking this test, check your answers against the answer key and score your test, but count only those questions that you answered without using the *Publication Manual*. If the total number of incorrect answers plus looked-up answers is 8 or more (20% or more incorrect), we advise you to complete all of the learning exercises. If you did well on the test (i.e., at least 36 of 41 correct), you may want to skip the learning exercises and take the practice test that follows these exercises or take a mastery test.

RESEARCH REPORT FAMILIARIZATION TEST

1. In contrast to empirical studies or theoretical articles, literature reviews

    a. define and clarify a problem.

    b. summarize previous investigations.

    c. identify relations, contradictions, or inconsistencies in the literature.

    d. suggest steps for future research.

    e. do all of the above.

2. Edit the following for typing the title page:

    CULTURAL INFLUENCES ON WILLINGNESS TO SEEK TREATMENT FOR SOCIAL ANXIETY
    IN CHINESE- AND EUROPEAN-HERITAGE STUDENTS

    Lorena Hsu and Lynn E. Alden
    University of British Columbia

    a. leave as is

    b.

    Cultural Influences on Willingness to Seek Treatment for Social Anxiety

    in Chinese- and European-Heritage Students

    Lorena Hsu and Lynn E. Alden

    University of British Columbia

    c.

    Cultural Influences on Willingness to Seek Treatment for Social Anxiety
    in Chinese- and European-Heritage Students

    Lorena Hsu & Lynn E. Alden
    University of British Columbia

    d.

    Cultural Influences on Willingness to Seek Treatment for Social Anxiety
    in Chinese- and European-Heritage Students

    Lorena Hsu   Lynn E. Alden
    University of British Columbia   University of British Columbia

3. Which of the following must identify the specific variables investigated and the relation between them?

    a. the first sentence of the introduction section

    b. the conclusion of the Discussion section

    c. the title of the report

    d. the first table that is cited

4. An abstract for a research report should be about

    a. 100 to 120 words.

    b. 75 to 100 words.

    c. 100 to 150 words.

    d. 150 to 180 words.

5. Journal article reporting standards were developed to

    a. make it easier to generalize across fields.

    b. provide a degree of comprehensiveness in the information routinely included in reports of empirical investigations.

    c. help decision makers in policy and practice understand how research was conducted and what was found.

    d. allow techniques of meta-analysis to proceed more efficiently.

    e. all of the above.

6. Conventionality and expediency dictate that the Method section should be written

    a. as a unified whole.

    b. in subsections.

    c. without reference notes.

    d. Answers a and c are correct.

    e. None of the above is correct.

7. When describing human participants, you should state

    a. the number of participants who did not complete the experiment.

    b. the total number of participants.

    c. the number of participants assigned to each experimental condition.

    d. all of the above.

    e. b and c of the above.

8. On the basis of verb tense, in which part of a report is the following text segment likely to appear?

    College students judge time differently than do college faculty. Faculty are more accurate in judging the amount of time required to do academic tasks.

    a. Method

    b. a review of the literature in an introduction

    c. a conclusion in a Discussion

    d. Results

9. In reporting tests of significance,

    a. give the exact value of the statistic (F or t value).

    b. state the relevant degrees of freedom.

    c. indicate the probability level.

    d. describe the direction of an effect.

    e. do all of the above.

10. If your study is simple and your Discussion section is brief and straightforward, you can

    a. discuss the flaws of the study at length.
    b. spend most of your time discussing the next study you plan to do.
    c. combine the Results and Discussion sections.
    d. discuss the negative findings, listing all of the possible causes.
    e. do all of the above.

11. Edit the following by selecting the correct arrangement of headings:

Experiment 1
Method

    Stimulus Materials
    Animal sounds.

a. leave as is

b.

Experiment 1

Method
    Stimulus materials.
    Animal sounds.

c.

Experiment 1

Method
    Stimulus materials.
    Animal sounds.

d.

EXPERIMENT 1
Method

    Stimulus Materials
    Animal sounds.

12. Approximations of quantity such as *a major portion of,* colloquial expressions such as *write-up,* or informal verb use such as *it was her feeling that*

    a. reduce word precision and clarity.
    b. add warmth to dull scientific prose.
    c. have a place in serious scientific writing.
    d. can be used to enhance communication.
    e. are more acceptable in written than in oral communication.

13. In table headings and figure captions,

    a. capitalize only the first word and proper nouns.
    b. capitalize all major words.
    c. do not capitalize any words.
    d. capitalization will depend on the message you wish to convey.

14. Names of conditions or groups in an experiment should

    a. be capitalized.
    b. not be capitalized.
    c. not be capitalized unless followed by numerals or letters.
    d. be designated by a letter.

15. Use italics for

    a. trigonometric terms.
    b. introduction of key terms and labels.
    c. Greek letters.
    d. all of the above.

16. Use numerals to express

    a. any number that begins a sentence.
    b. common fractions.
    c. numbers that immediately precede a unit of measurement.
    d. none of the above.

17. Edit the following for the expression of numbers:

    Respondents in each of the age groups were asked to describe what they had eaten for dinner two and four weeks previously.

    a. leave as is
    b. Respondents in each of the age groups were asked to describe what they had eaten for dinner 2 and 4 weeks previously.
    c. Respondents in each of the age groups were asked to describe what they had eaten for dinner two (2) and four (4) weeks previously.

18. Edit the following for the expression of numbers:

    Eighty nurses volunteered to keep a daily record of their stress levels.

    a. leave as is
    b. 80 nurses volunteered to keep a daily record of their stress levels.
    c. Eighty (80) nurses volunteered to keep a daily record of their stress levels.

19. Words should be used to express numbers

    a. whenever numbers are greater than 20 but less than 200.
    b. from zero to nine, not representing a precise measurement.
    c. always, except when cardinal numbers have satisfied the requirements of ratio measurement and are grouped for comparison with themselves.
    d. as seldom as possible.

20. Edit the following for the expression of ordinal numbers:

    The critical stimuli were placed in the second and 10th positions in each block of trials.

    a. leave as is
    b. The critical stimuli were placed in the 2nd and 10th positions in each block of trials.
    c. The critical stimuli were placed in the second and tenth positions in each block of trials.

21. Edit the following for the expression of decimal fractions:

    The containers were made of transparent plastic and weighed .6 kg.

    a. leave as is
    b. The containers were made of transparent plastic and weighed 0.6 kg.
    c. The containers were made of transparent plastic and weighed 6×10^{-1} kg.
    d. The containers were made of transparent plastic and weighed 60×10^{-2} kg.

22. Edit the following for the expression of numbers:

    When the payoff for finding an effective treatment is so high, it is important to minimize Type 2 errors.

    a. leave as is
    b. When the payoff for finding an effective treatment is so high, it is important to minimize Type II errors.
    c. When the payoff for finding an effective treatment is so high, it is important to minimize Type Two errors.

23. Use commas between groups of three digits in figures of 1,000 or more except when expressing

    a. page numbers.
    b. serial numbers.
    c. degrees of freedom.
    d. all of the above.

24. Which statement applies to the use of metric measurement in the following sentence?

    Conductance and inductance were measured in Siemens (S) and henrys (H), respectively.

    a. correct as is
    b. The measurements do not conform to the International System of Units.
    c. Measurements should not be expressed in metric units in social or behavioral science journals.
    d. Inductance should be measured in newtons per meter, not in henrys.

25. When you present statistics, cite the reference

    a. for less common statistics.
    b. for statistics used in a controversial way.
    c. when a statistic itself is the focus of an article.
    d. for all of the above.
    e. for any statistics and all uses of a statistic.

26. Edit the following for the expression of formulas:

    The participants were told their mean reaction times (M = total reaction time/number of trials) after each block of trials.

    a. leave as is
    b. The participants were told their mean reaction times (M = SRT/n trials) after each block of trials.
    c. The participants were told their mean reaction times $[M = (\text{RT}_1 + \text{RT}_2 + \text{RT}_3 \ldots + \text{RT}_n)\, n_\text{T}]$ after each block of trials.
    d. The participants were told their mean reaction times after each block of trials.

27. Which of the following is the correct way to present a statistic in text?

    a. $F = 2.62(22), p<.01$
    b. $t(22) = 2.62, p <. 01$
    c. $t = 2.62(22), p <. 01$
    d. none of the above

28. Edit the following for the presentation of statistics:

    The children were divided into two groups on the basis of which hand they used to hold the pen. The mean scores on the orientation task for the two groups were 34 and 142.

    a. leave as is
    b. The children were divided into two groups on the basis of which hand they used to hold the pen. The mean scores on the orientation task for the left-handed and right-handed groups were 34 and 142, respectively.
    c. The children were divided into two groups on the basis of which hand they used to hold the pen. The mean scores on the orientation task for the left-handed and right-handed groups were 34 and 142.
    d. The children were divided into two groups on the basis of which hand they used to hold the pen. The mean scores on the orientation task for the two groups were 34 and 142, respectively.

29. Edit the following for the presentation of statistical symbols:

    For immediate recognition, the omnibus test of the main effect of sentence format was statistically significant, $F(2, 177) = 6.30$, $p=.002$, est. $\omega^2=.07$.

    a. leave as is
    b. For immediate recognition, the omnibus test of the main effect of sentence format was statistically significant, $F(2/177) = 6.30$, $p = 0.002$, est. $\omega^2 = .07$.
    c. For immediate recognition, the omnibus test of the main effect of sentence format was statistically significant, $F[2,177] = 6.30$, $p = .002$, est. $\omega^2 = .07$.
    d. For immediate recognition, the omnibus test of the main effect of sentence format was statistically significant, $F(2, 177) = 6.30$, $p = .002$, est. $\omega^2 = .07$.

30. Tables should be numbered in the order

    a. that puts the longest table first.
    b. in which they are first mentioned in the text.
    c. that seems most logical to the author.
    d. that seems most logical to an editor.

31. Before constructing a table, you should consider that

    a. different indices should be segregated into different parts or lines of tables.
    b. tables with surplus elements are less effective than lean tables.
    c. data from a 2 × 2 design should be put in a table rather than in the text.
    d. adding space between columns or rows can make a table easier to read.
    e. all of the above except c.

32. A good table

    a. is intelligible without reference to the text.
    b. does not need to be discussed in the text.
    c. duplicates information in the text.
    d. does a and b.

33. The left-hand column of a table (the stub) should have a heading (the stub head) that usually describes the

    a. elements in that column.
    b. dependent variables.
    c. independent variables.
    d. data.
    e. a and c.

34. When more than one level of significance is reported in a table,

    a. each level is represented by a single asterisk.
    b. assign the same number of asterisks from table to table within your paper.
    c. report the exact probabilities to two to three decimal places.
    d. b and c.

35. From the following examples, select the correct way to refer to a figure in text;

    a. see the figure above
    b. see the figure on page 14
    c. see Figure 2
    d. see Figure 2 above on page 14

36. Tables, including titles and headings, should be

    a. triple-spaced.
    b. double-spaced.
    c. single-spaced.
    d. b or c.

37. The word *figure* refers to

    a. photographs.
    b. graphs and charts.
    c. maps.
    d. all of the above.

38. Figures can be used to

    a. illustrate complex theoretical formulations.
    b. show sampling and flow of subjects through a randomized clinical trial or other experiment.
    c. illustrate empirical results from a complex multivariate model.
    d. all of the above.

39. Which of the following is the correct ordering of manuscript subsections?

    a. title page, introduction, abstract, text
    b. References, appendices, author identification notes
    c. Method, Discussion, Results
    d. figures, figure captions, tables
    e. Discussion, footnotes, References

40. The title page of your manuscript includes

    a. running head.
    b. author byline.
    c. author note.
    d. all of the above.

41. The abstract should

    a. appear on the same page above the title and introduction.
    b. be single-spaced and set with larger margins.
    c. begin on page 2.
    d. be no longer than 3% of the text.

RESEARCH REPORT FAMILIARIZATION TEST
ANSWER SHEET AND FEEDBACK REPORT

Student Name _____ Date _____

Question Number	Answer	APA Codes	Question Number	Answer	APA Codes
1	_____	1.01–1.06	22	_____	4.31–4.38
2	_____	2.01–2.03	23	_____	4.31–4.38
3	_____	2.01–2.03	24	_____	4.39–4.40
4	_____	2.01–2.04	25	_____	4.41–4.47
5	_____	2.01–2.13	26	_____	4.41–4.47
6	_____	2.05–2.06	27	_____	4.41–4.47
7	_____	2.05–2.06	28	_____	4.41–4.47
8	_____	2.05–2.08	29	_____	4.41–4.47
9	_____	2.07–2.11	30	_____	5.05
10	_____	2.07–2.11	31	_____	5.07–5.17
11	_____	3.02–3.03	32	_____	5.07–5.17
12	_____	3.08–3.09	33	_____	5.07–5.17
13	_____	4.14–4.20	34	_____	5.07–5.17
14	_____	4.14–4.20	35	_____	5.10
15	_____	4.21	36	_____	5.17
16	_____	4.31–4.38	37	_____	5.20–5.30
17	_____	4.31–4.38	38	_____	5.20–5.30
18	_____	4.31–4.38	39	_____	8.03
19	_____	4.31–4.38	40	_____	8.03
20	_____	4.31–4.38	41	_____	8.03
21	_____	4.31–4.38			

NUMBER CORRECT _____

RESEARCH REPORT FAMILIARIZATION TEST
ANSWER KEY

Question Number	Answer	APA Codes	Question Number	Answer	APA Codes
1	e	1.01–1.06	22	b	4.31–4.38
2	b	2.01–2.03	23	d	4.31–4.38
3	c	2.01–2.03	24	a	4.39–4.40
4	d	2.01–2.04	25	d	4.41–4.47
5	e	2.01–2.13	26	d	4.41–4.47
6	b	2.05–2.06	27	d	4.41–4.47
7	d	2.05–2.06	28	b	4.41–4.47
8	c	2.05–2.08	29	d	4.41–4.47
9	e	2.07–2.11	30	b	5.05
10	c	2.07–2.11	31	e	5.07–5.17
11	b	3.02–3.03	32	a	5.07–5.17
12	a	3.08–3.09	33	e	5.07–5.17
13	a	4.14–4.20	34	d	5.07–5.17
14	c	4.14–4.20	35	c	5.10
15	b	4.21	36	d	5.17
16	c	4.31–4.38	37	d	5.20–5.30
17	b	4.31–4.38	38	d	5.20–5.30
18	a	4.31–4.38	39	e	8.03
19	b	4.31–4.38	40	d	8.03
20	a	4.31–4.38	41	c	8.03
21	b	4.31–4.38			

Research Report Learning Exercises and Integrative Exercises

There are two types of exercises: learning and integrative. *Learning exercises* are brief excerpts of text that address one or two components of APA style (e.g., metrication, numbers). *Integrative exercises* consist of a paragraph or page of text that you are to edit. The learning exercises and integrative exercises appear in two versions: draft (incorrect) and feedback (correct). The feedback and draft versions appear on the left- and right-hand pages, respectively. There are APA codes under each section title as well as below each exercise; these codes correspond to the relevant sections in the *Publication Manual*.

In learning exercises, the components that are being targeted (i.e., in need of correction) are shaded. Read the text of the draft version on the right-hand page and decide whether the shaded text is correct or incorrect. Write corrections on the workbook page directly above the errors. You may consult the *Publication Manual* at any time. Check your answers against the feedback version on the left-hand page to see whether your answer is correct. The feedback version will state "correct as is," or the correctly edited material will be shaded.

In integrative exercises, the components in need of correction are not shaded, but the errors in each exercise are all related to the style rules applied in the preceding group of learning exercises. Read the text carefully, and edit the text, marking corrections directly on the draft version. The corrections on the feedback page are shaded. Integrative exercises appear at the end of each group of learning exercises.

Headings and Series
APA Codes: 3.02–3.04

NOTES:

Method

Participants
Materials
Procedure

Results
Discussion
References

APA CODES: 3.02–3.03

Participants
Procedure

    Early experience.
    Experimental training.
    Testing.

Results
Discussion
References

APA CODES: 3.02–3.03

Headings and Series
APA Codes: 3.02–3.04

These exercises cover organizing a manuscript with headings, levels of headings, selecting the levels of headings, and seriation (see the *Publication Manual,* sections 3.02–3.04). Mark corrections directly on the right-hand page and compare your responses with the correct answers on the left-hand page. When you are finished with this section, go on to the next section on which you need practice.

Introduction

Method

Participants

Materials

Procedure

Results

Discussion

References

APA CODES: 3.02–3.03

Method

Participants

Procedure

    Early experience.

    Experimental training.

    Testing.

Results

Discussion

References

APA CODES: 3.02–3.03

Experiment 1

Method

    Participants.

    Materials.

    Client descriptions.

    Rating scales.

    Procedure.

    Assessment training.

    Client familiarization.

    Client evaluation.

Results

Discussion

Experiment 2

Method

    Participants.

    Materials.

    Procedure.

Results

Discussion

General Discussion
References

Correct as is.

APA CODES: 3.02–3.03

Stimulus materials. The four episodes evaluated by the different groups were identical except for the descriptions of the client's history and the behavior that led to the client being brought to the therapist.

APA CODE: 3.03

Experiment 1

Method

    Participants.

    Materials.

    Client descriptions.

    Rating scales.

    Procedure.

    Assessment training.

    Client familiarization.

    Client evaluation.

Results

Discussion

Experiment 2

Method

    Participants.

    Materials.

    Procedure.

Results

Discussion

General Discussion

References

APA CODES: 3.02–3.03

Stimulus Materials. The four episodes evaluated by the different groups were identical except for the descriptions of the client's history and the behavior that led to the client being brought to the therapist.

APA CODE: 3.03

Method

Subjects

Captive animals. The subjects were 96 nocturnal mammals from a zoo in Canada and another 96 nocturnal mammals from a zoo in Australia.

APA CODE: 3.03

Method

Subjects

Procedure

Treatment.

Immediate evaluation.

Delayed evaluation.

Results

Discussion

References

APA CODES: 3.02–3.03

Prior to being timed on the test puzzle, the respondents had one of five experiences with a similar puzzle: (a) watched an expert solve the puzzle, (b) watched a novice solve the puzzle, (c) solved the puzzle alone, (d) looked at the puzzle without working on it, and (e) had no experience.

APA CODE: 3.04

Method

Subjects:

Captive Animals: The subjects were 96 nocturnal mammals from a zoo in Canada and another 96 nocturnal mammals from a zoo in Australia.

APA CODE: 3.03

METHOD

Subjects

Procedure

    Treatment:

    Immediate Evaluation: Delayed

    Evaluation:

RESULTS

DISCUSSION

REFERENCES

APA CODES: 3.02–3.03

Prior to being timed on the test puzzle, the respondents had one of five experiences with a similar puzzle: (1) watched an expert solve the puzzle, (2) watched a novice solve the puzzle, (3) solved the puzzle alone, (4) looked at the puzzle without working on it, and (5) had no experience.

APA CODE: 3.04

All participants underwent the same sequence of events:
1. They completed a form anonymously that provided demographic information.
2. They filled out the Multiple Affect Adjective Check List (MAACL).
3. They completed the sex role inventory.
4. They observed the videotape appropriate for the condition to which the subject had been assigned.
5. They filled out the MAACL again.

Correct as is.

APA CODE: 3.04

The adolescents were divided into 18 groups according to whether they selected a role model who was (a) Black, White, or Hispanic; (b) male or female; and (c) an athlete, entertainer, or scientist.

APA CODE: 3.04

Method

Participants

APA CODE: 3.03

All participants underwent the same sequence of events:
1. They completed a form anonymously that provided demographic information.
2. They filled out the Multiple Affect Adjective Check List (MAACL).
3. They completed the sex role inventory.
4. They observed the videotape appropriate for the condition to which the subject had been assigned.
5. They filled out the MAACL again.

APA CODE: 3.04

The adolescents were divided into 18 groups according to whether they selected a role model who was (a) Black, White, or Hispanic, (b) male or female, and (c) an athlete, entertainer, or scientist.

APA CODE: 3.04

METHOD

Participants

APA CODE: 3.03

Integrative Exercise: Headings and Series

Experiment 2

In Experiment 1, the gender of another person was shown to affect a child's expectations of the behavior of that person. We conducted Experiment 2 for three purposes:

1. One goal was to test whether the gender-based expectations identified in Experiment 1 depend on the age of the other person.

2. If age of the object-person is a mediating factor, then a second purpose was to determine whether the expectations of the behavior of boys or girls change more with the age of the object-person.

3. Our final goal was to determine how the behavior of children toward another person changes as a function of the age of the other person, regardless of the gender of the other person.

Method

Respondents. The respondents were one hundred twenty 4-year-old boys and one hundred twenty 4-year-old girls attending nursery schools in the urban and suburban sections of a major city. None of the children who had participated in Experiment 1 participated in Experiment 2. Informed consent for the child's participation was obtained from the parent or legal guardian of each child who participated.

Design. The experiment was a $2 \times 2 \times 4$ between-subjects design. The sex of the respondent was a selected variable. The sex and age (8, 12, 20, and 60 years old) of the storyteller to whom each child was assigned was manipulated. Fifteen girls and 15 boys were randomly assigned to each of the eight (Sex × Age) storyteller conditions.

Procedure

Storytellers and storyteller training. The 20-year-old storytellers were the same two people who served as storytellers in Experiment 1. The 8- and 12-year-old storytellers were two girls and two boys who were recommended by their teachers and school librarian on the basis of their avid interest in reading and their skills in reading aloud. The 60-year-old storytellers were a man and a woman who served as literacy volunteers and volunteer readers in the children's program of the local public library. The storytellers were trained following the same procedures as were used in Experiment 1.

APA CODES: 3.02–3.04

Integrative Exercise: Headings and Series
Experiment 2
Introduction

In Experiment 1, the gender of another person was shown to affect a child's expectations of the behavior of that person. We conducted Experiment 2 for three purposes:

1. One goal was to test whether the gender-based expectations identified in Experiment 1 depend on the age of the other person.

2. If age of the object-person is a mediating factor, then a second purpose was to determine whether the expectations of the behavior of boys or girls change more with the age of the object-person.

3. Our final goal was to determine how the behavior of children toward another person changes as a function of the age of the other person, regardless of the gender of the other person.

Method

Respondents: The respondents were one hundred twenty 4-year-old boys and one hundred twenty 4-year-old girls attending nursery schools in the urban and suburban sections of a major city. None of the children who had participated in Experiment 1 participated in Experiment 2. Informed consent for the child's participation was obtained from the parent or legal guardian of each child who participated.

Design: The experiment was a 2 × 2 × 4 between-subjects design. The sex of the respondent was a selected variable. The sex and age (8, 12, 20, and 60 years old) of the storyteller to whom each child was assigned was manipulated. Fifteen girls and 15 boys were randomly assigned to each of the eight (Sex × Age) storyteller conditions.

Procedure

Storytellers and Storyteller Training: The 20-year-old storytellers were the same two people who served as storytellers in Experiment 1. The 8- and 12-year-old storytellers were two girls and two boys who were recommended by their teachers and school librarian on the basis of their avid interest in reading and their skills in reading aloud. The 60-year-old storytellers were a man and a woman who served as literacy volunteers and volunteer readers in the children's program of the local public library. The storytellers were trained following the same procedures as were used in Experiment 1.

APA CODES: 3.02–3.04

Capitalization
APA Codes: 4.14–4.20

NOTES:

On the 3rd day of Experiment 2, the children read Chapter 6 of their sex education text. Then there was a discussion about sexual transmission of disease.

APA CODE: 4.17

As can be seen in Table 9 and Figure 2, clients who were misinformed about sex as children were also more likely to believe in sexual myths as adults.

APA CODE: 4.17

The control groups were counterbalanced across both Condition A and Condition B.

APA CODE: 4.19

Participants in the tobacco-chewing therapy condition and the no-therapy control condition then received two wads of chewing tobacco.

APA CODE: 4.19

Sarcastic sentences were remembered better than nonsarcastic sentences; however, there was no Sarcasm × Sex × Self- Esteem interaction effect.

APA CODE: 4.20

An analysis of variance showed that the between-subjects variable was significant.

APA CODE: 4.20

Integrative Exercise: Capitalization

On Trial 26 of Experiment 9, Boreal owls *(Aegolius funereus)* were reintroduced as pets in the huts of those elderly Algonquins who were assigned to the therapy condition. Feather dusters were given to the control groups to assess placebo effects. After 2 weeks of contact with the feathered stimuli, all participants received the Peck Reality Orientation Scale.

APA CODES: 4.14–4.20

Capitalization
APA Codes: 4.14–4.20

These exercises cover capitalization of (a) nouns followed by numerals or letters; (b) titles of tests; (c) names of conditions or groups in an experiment; and (d) names of factors, variables, and effects (see the *Publication Manual,* sections 4.14–4.20). Mark corrections directly on the right-hand page, and compare your responses with the correct answers on the left-hand page. When you are finished with this section, go on to the next section on which you need practice.

On the third day of experiment 2, the children read chapter 6 of their sex education text. Then there was a discussion about sexual transmission of disease.

APA CODE: 4.17

As can be seen in table 9 and figure *2,* clients who were misinformed about sex as children were also more likely to believe in sexual myths as adults.

APA CODE: 4.17

The Control Groups were counterbalanced across both condition A and condition B.

APA CODE: 4.19

Participants in the tobacco-chewing therapy condition and the No-Therapy control condition then received two wads of chewing tobacco.

APA CODE: 4.19

Sarcastic sentences were remembered better than nonsarcastic sentences; however, there was no sarcasm X sex X self-esteem interaction effect.

APA CODE: 4.20

An analysis of variance showed that the between-subjects factor was significant.

APA CODE: 4.20

Integrative Exercise: Capitalization

On trial 26 of Experiment 9, boreal owls *(Aegolius funereus)* were reintroduced as pets in the huts of those elderly Algonquins who were assigned to the Therapy Condition. Feather dusters were given to the control groups to assess Placebo Effects. After 2 Weeks of contact with the feathered stimuli, all participants received the Peck reality orientation scale.

APA CODES: 4.14–4.20

Abbreviations
APA Codes: 4.22–4.30

NOTES:

The Minnesota Multiphasic Personality Inventory (MMPI) was administered to respondents of different handedness, 26 left-handed and 62 right-handed.

APA CODES: 4.22, 4.25

Three kinds of odor tests were presented to college students: odor recognition (OR), odor discrimination (OD), and odor matching (OM). Tests were administered in either the OD–OR–OM or OM–OR–OD sequence.

Correct as is.

APA CODES: 4.22–4.23

Low doses of LSD seemed to have no effect on the ESP of pygmy chimpanzees.

Correct as is.

APA CODE: 4.24

Integrative Exercise: Abbreviations

IQ tests were administered to 480 subjects who had recently completed BA, MA, or PhD degrees in psychology. All of the students were then given the General Aptitude in Psychology (GAP) test. As predicted, no effects of education were observed with either the IQ or the GAP test as the criterion measure (i.e., BA, MA, and PhD students were not different in either intelligence or aptitude).

APA CODES: 4.22–4.30

Abbreviations
APA Codes: 4.22–4.30

These exercises cover the use of abbreviations, explaining abbreviations, abbreviations accepted as words, abbreviations used in APA journals, Latin abbreviations, abbreviations of units of measurement and statistics, use of periods with abbreviations, plurals of abbreviations, and abbreviations beginning a sentence (see the *Publication Manual,* sections 4.22–4.30). Mark corrections directly on the right-hand page, and compare your responses with the correct answers on the left-hand page. When you are finished with this section, go on to the next section on which you need practice.

The MMPI was administered to respondents of different handedness, 26 LH and 62 RH.

APA CODES: 4.22, 4.25

Three kinds of odor tests were presented to college students: odor recognition (OR), odor discrimination (OD), and odor matching (OM). Tests were administered in either the OD–OR–OM or OM–OR–OD sequence.

APA CODES: 4.22–4.23

Low doses of LSD seemed to have no effect on the ESP of pygmy chimpanzees.

APA CODE: 4.24

Integrative Exercise: Abbreviations

Intelligence quotient tests were administered to 480 Ss who recently completed BA, MA, or Ph.D. degrees in psychology. All of the students were then given the General Aptitude in Psychology (GAP) test. As predicted, no effects of education were observed with either the IQ or the General Aptitude in Psychology (GAP) test as the criterion measure (i.e., BA, MA, and Ph.D. students were not different in either intelligence or aptitude).

APA CODES: 4.22–4.30

Numbers
APA Codes: 4.31–4.38

NOTES:

The inventory consists of 30 personal characteristics to be rated by the respondent.

APA CODE: 4.31

In nine of those studies, women scored higher; in seven, men scored higher; and in the other 12, no reliable differences between men and women were observed.

APA CODE: 4.31

Before the children were given the test weights to judge, 20 children were asked to move 10 blocks that weighed 1 kg each and 20 children were asked to move 10 blocks that weighed 4 kg each.

APA CODE: 4.29

Pounds of weight loss was recorded as the dependent variable, and hours spent with the phobic object was the independent variable.

APA CODE: 4.30

Numbers
APA Codes: 4.31–4.38

These exercises give you practice in using numbers expressed as numerals, numbers expressed in words, combining figures and words to express numbers, ordinal numbers, decimal fractions, Arabic or Roman numerals, commas in numbers, and plurals of numbers (see the *Publication Manual,* sections 4.31–4.38). Mark corrections directly on the right-hand page, and compare your responses with the correct answers on the left-hand page. When you are finished with this section, go on to the next section on which you need practice.

The inventory consists of thirty personal characteristics to be rated by the respondent.

APA CODE: 4.31

In nine of those studies, women scored higher; in seven, men scored higher; and in the other twelve, no reliable differences between men and women were observed.

APA CODE: 4.31

Before the children were given the test weights to judge, 20 children were asked to move 10 blocks that weighed 1 kg each and 20 children were asked to move 10 blocks that weighed 4 kgs each.

APA CODE: 4.29

lbs of weight loss was recorded as the dependent variable, and hours spent with the phobic object was the independent variable.

APA CODE: 4.30

Each child read four stories and answered 12 reading comprehension questions about each story.

APA CODE: 4.31

Minority group characters were portrayed as responsible for the solution of a problem in only 6% of the episodes in which they appeared.

Correct as is.

APA CODE: 4.31

The clients were returned to the clinic for assessment 1 week and 5 weeks after the last group therapy session.

Correct as is.

APA CODE: 4.31

Because of mechanical failure, participants' scores on the 7-point scale were eliminated.

APA CODE: 4.31

The greatest increase in responding was between Trial 2 and Trial 3.

APA CODE: 4.31

The sketches presented to the different groups contained 2, 3, 4, 5, and 6 facial features, respectively.

APA CODE: 4.31

Each set of letters could be arranged to form either of two words.

Correct as is

APA CODE: 4.32

A total of 53 clients volunteered. Forty were selected on the basis of clinical histories and treatment to date.

APA CODE: 4.32

There were 16 pictures in each condition. Eight pictures were of familiar people, and eight were of unfamiliar people.

Correct as is.

APA CODE: 4.32

Each child read 4 stories and answered 12 reading comprehension questions about each story.

APA CODE: 4.31

Minority group characters were portrayed as responsible for the solution of a problem in only 6% of the episodes in which they appeared.

APA CODE: 4.31

The clients were returned to the clinic for assessment 1 week and 5 weeks after the last group therapy session.

APA CODE: 4.31

Because of mechanical failure, participants' scores on the seven-point scale were eliminated.

APA CODE: 4.31

The greatest increase in responding was between Trial Two and Trial Three.

APA CODE: 4.31

The sketches presented to the different groups contained two, three, four, five, and six facial features, respectively.

APA CODE: 4.31

Each set of letters could be arranged to form either of two words.

APA CODE: 4.32

A total of 53 clients volunteered. 40 were selected on the basis of clinical histories and treatment to date.

APA CODE: 4.32

There were 16 pictures in each condition. Eight pictures were of familiar people, and eight were of unfamiliar people.

APA CODE: 4.32

In the conjunctive condition, the group could not go on to the next step until at least three fourths of the group members had mastered the previous step.

APA CODE: 4.32

Each story was read to fifteen 5-year-olds and fifteen 8-year-olds.

APA CODE: 4.33

The first block of trials was a practice set.
Correct as is.

APA CODE: 4.34

The third graders and fifth graders were given a rest after the 20th trial in each block.

APA CODE: 4.34

The mean number of absences by the 24 students was 3.7.

APA CODE: 4.35

The greater the number of people who viewed the program together, the poorer was their memory for details ($r = -.63$).

APA CODE: 4.35

The procedure for Experiment 2 was identical to that used in Experiment 1, except that the child did not receive feedback after each trial.

APA CODE: 4.36

The participants were shown real or fabricated newspaper stories that had appeared in the 1970s, 1980s, or 1990s.

APA CODE: 4.38

In the conjunctive condition, the group could not go on to the next step until at least 3/4 of the group members had mastered the previous step.

APA CODE: 4.32

Each story was read to 15 5-year-olds and 15 8-year-olds.

APA CODE: 4.33

The first block of trials was a practice set.

APA CODE: 4.34

The 3rd graders and 5th graders were given a rest after the 20th trial in each block.

APA CODE: 4.34

The mean number of absences by the 24 students was 3.6666667.

APA CODE: 4.35

The greater the number of people who viewed the program together, the poorer was their memory for details ($r = -0.63$).

APA CODE: 4.35

The procedure for Experiment II was identical to that used in Experiment I, except that the child did not receive feedback after each trial.

APA CODE: 4.36

The participants were shown real or fabricated newspaper stories that had appeared in the 1970's, 1980's, or 1990's.

APA CODE: 4.38

Integrative Exercise: Numbers

Food supply was expected to affect aggression, but it was not clear what effect it would have on jumping behavior. Musical upbringing was expected to affect jumping behavior but not aggression, especially when food was abundant. No long-term effects of either variable were expected.

Method

Subjects

Ninety-six frogs were selected from the frog pool of the Calaveras County Jumping Academy. An expert judged their ages to be between 8 and 60 days since emerging from their tadpole state. Direct measurements indicated that the thickness of their rear-upper legs ranged from 0.65 cm to 4.85 cm.

Design

A 2 × 3 factorial design was used to manipulate the food supply (limited or abundant) and the musical environment (rock and roll, popular, or classical) of the frogs. Groups of six frogs, matched within 0.05 cm on thickness of rear-upper legs, were randomly assigned to the six conditions, resulting in the assignment of 16 frogs to each condition.

Apparatus

Seven identical enclosed, air-conditioned habitats were constructed, each containing a grassy area surrounding a pond. The pond contained pond water ranging in depth from 0.1 m to 2.7 m, pond mud at the bottom, numerous rocks and lily pads, and other vegetation found in the frogs' natural habitat.

Procedure

The 16 frogs that were assigned to a particular condition were placed in one-of the six identical habitats and kept there for a total of 8 weeks, except for individual testing (as described in the next paragraph), which was conducted in the seventh habitat. The frogs in the six experimental conditions received different treatments during Days 1–14. In the limited-supply habitats, 400 flies were introduced daily; in the abundant-supply habitats, 1,600 flies were introduced daily. In each habitat, music periods lasting for a 2-hr duration alternated with quiet periods lasting 2 hr. The music was piped in over loudspeakers. Eight selections, each lasting 0.25 hr, were chosen for the rock-and-roll, popular, and classical conditions. Appendix A contains the list of specific selections for each musical condition. For each condition, six different tape recordings of the eight selections in a different random order were made. Each of the six tapes was piped into the habitat during one of the six music periods each day.

Each frog was observed in its group habitat by three observers for 5 min on Day 14. The observers (who were blind to the experimental condition—they wore headphones over which bullfrog croakings were played to mask the musical condition) counted the number of aggressive acts, the number of jumps, and the length of the longest jump (the starting and landing spots were marked on a sketch of the habitat, and jump length was later converted to distance in meters using a blueprint of the habitat) by the frog being observed.

APA CODES: 4.31–4.38

Integrative Exercise: Numbers

Food supply was expected to affect aggression, but it was not clear what effect it would have on jumping behavior. Musical upbringing was expected to affect jumping behavior but not aggression, especially when food was abundant. No long-term effects of either variable were expected.

Method

Subjects

96 frogs were selected from the frog pool of the Calaveras County Jumping Academy. An expert judged their ages to be between eight and 60 days since emerging from their tadpole state. Direct measurements indicated that the thickness of their rear-upper legs ranged from .65 cm to 4.85 cm.

Design

A 2 × 3 factorial design was used to manipulate the food supply (limited or abundant) and the musical environment (rock and roll, popular, or classical) of the frogs. Groups of 6 frogs, matched within 0.05 cm on thickness of rear-upper legs, were randomly assigned to the six conditions, resulting in the assignment of 16 frogs to each condition.

Apparatus

Seven identical enclosed, air-conditioned habitats were constructed, each containing a grassy area surrounding a pond. The pond contained pond water ranging in depth from .1m to 2.7 m, pond mud at the bottom, numerous rocks and lily pads, and other vegetation found in the frogs' natural habitat.

Procedure

The sixteen frogs that were assigned to a particular condition were placed in one of the 6 identical habitats and kept there for a total of 8 weeks, except for individual testing (as described in the next paragraph), which was conducted in the 7th habitat. The frogs in the six experimental conditions received different treatments during Days 1–14. In the limited-supply habitats, 400 flies were introduced daily; in the abundant-supply habitats, 1600 flies were introduced daily. In each habitat, music periods lasting for a two-hr duration alternated with quiet periods lasting two hr. The music was piped in over loudspeakers. Eight selections, each lasting 0.25 hr, were chosen for the rock-and-roll, popular, and classical conditions. Appendix I contains the list of specific selections for each musical condition. For each condition, 6 different tape recordings of the eight selections in a different random order were made. Each of the 6 tapes was piped into the habitat during one of the six music periods each day.

Each frog was observed in its group habitat by 3 observers for five min on Day 14. The observers (who were blind to the experimental condition—they wore headphones over which bullfrog croakings were played to mask the musical condition) counted the number of aggressive acts, the number of jumps, and the length of the longest jump (the starting and landing spots were marked on a sketch of the habitat, and jump length was later converted to distance in meters using a blueprint of the habitat) by the frog being observed.

APA CODES: 4.31–4.38

Metrication
APA Codes: 4.39–4.40

NOTES:

Cross-sex pairs of students were placed face-to-face 1.5 ft (0.45 m) apart.

APA CODE: 4.39

The amount of time it took respondents to blush when embarrassed was 1.4 s.

APA CODE: 4.40

Rats in the binge-training condition weighed an average of 16 kg; this represented a 600% increase in weight.

APA CODE: 4.40

Integrative Exercise: Metrication

The alleged ESP signals were transmitted 30 ft (9.1 m) by participants said to possess telepathic power. Participants claiming to have psychokinetic powers attempted to slide a 1.2-kg puck across a 0.001-m line. Those who believed themselves to have precognition ability had to guess the identity of playing cards 10 s before the cards were revealed. Finally, with the participants said to have had out-of-body experiences, spiritual transfer was measured in henrys per meter (H/m). Ambient electromagnetic radiation was reduced by placing the participants in a 7-m by 7-m lead cubicle. The lead walls were 1 ft (0.30) m thick.

APA CODES: 4.39–4.40

Metrication
APA Codes: 4.39–4.40

These exercises cover APA's policy on metrication, the style for metric units, and metric tables (see the *Publication Manual*, sections 4.39–4.40). Mark corrections directly on the right-hand page, and compare your responses with the correct answers on the left-hand page. When you are finished with this section, go on to the next section in which you need practice.

Cross-sex pairs of students were placed face-to-face 1.5 ft apart.

APA CODE: 4.39

The amount of time it took respondents to blush when embarrassed was 1.4 sec.

APA CODE: 4.40

Rats in the binge-training condition weighed an average of 16 K.G.; this represented a 600% increase in weight.

APA CODE: 4.40

Integrative Exercise: Metrication

The alleged ESP signals were transmitted 30 ft by participants said to possess telepathic power. Participants claiming to have psychokinetic powers attempted to slide a 1.2-k g puck across a 0.001-m line. Those who believed themselves to have precognition ability had to guess the identity of playing cards 10 secs. before the cards were revealed. Finally, with the participants said to have had out-of-body experiences, spiritual transfer was measured in henrys per meter (H/m). Ambient electromagnetic radiation was reduced by placing the participants in a 7-m by 7-m lead cubicle. The lead walls were 1 ft thick.

APA CODES: 4.39–4.40

Statistical and Mathematical Copy
APA Codes: 4.41–4.51

NOTES:

A 2 × 2 between-subjects analysis of variance was performed on the judgment scores.

APA CODE: 4.42

A one-way analysis of variance indicated no effect of the different types of training.

APA CODE: 4.43

The one-degree-of-freedom contrast of primary interest (the mean difference between Conditions 1 and 2) was also statistically significant at the specified .05 level, $t(177) = 3.51$, $p < .001$, $d = 0.65$, 95% CI [0.35, 0.95].

APA CODE: 4.44

Testing in their native language led to higher scores ($M = 84.2$, $SD = 3.6$) than did testing in English ($M = 77.4$, $SD = 2.1$), $t(58) = 3.7$, $p < .01$.

APA CODE: 4.44

For immediate recognition, the omnibus test of the main effect of sentence format was statistically significant, $F(2, 177) = 6.30$, $p = .002$, est. $\omega^2 = .07$.

APA CODE: 4.44

The analysis of variance indicated an effect of training style, $F(1, 75) = 9.8$, $p < .001$.

APA CODE: 4.44

Also reported were the 95% confidence intervals (CI) [5.62, 8.31], [−2.43, 4.31], and [−4.29, −3.11], respectively.

APA CODE: 4.44

Statistical and Mathematical Copy
APA Codes: 4.41–4.51

These exercises cover (a) selecting the method of data analysis and retaining data; (b) selecting effective presentation of statistics; (c) references for statistics; (d) formulas; (e) statistics in text; (f) statistical symbols; (g) spacing, alignment, and punctuation; (h) equations in text; and (i) displayed equations (see the *Publication Manual,* sections 4.41–4.51). Mark corrections directly on the right-hand page, and compare your responses with the correct answers on the left-hand page. When you are finished with this section, go on to the next section on which you need practice.

A 2 × 2 between-subjects analysis of variance (Winer, 1971) was performed on the judgment scores.

APA CODE: 4.42

A one-way analysis of variance ($F = MS_T/MS_E$) indicated no effect of the different types of training.

APA CODE: 4.43

The one-degree-of-freedom contrast of primary interest (the mean difference between Conditions 1 and 2) was also statistically significant at the specified .05 level, $t_{177} = 3.51$, $p < .001$, $d = 0.65$, 95% CI [0.35, 0.95].

APA CODE: 4.44

Testing in their native language led to higher scores ($\bar{X} = 84.2$, SD = 3.6) than did testing in English ($\bar{X} = 77.4$ SD = 2.1), $t(58) = 3.7$, $p < .01$.

APA CODE: 4.44

For immediate recognition, the omnibus test of the main effect of sentence format was statistically significant, $F(2/177) = 6.30$, $p = .002$, est. $\omega^2 = .07$.

APA CODE: 4.44

The analysis of variance indicated an effect of training style, F = 9.8, df= 1/75, $p < .001$.

APA CODE: 4.44

Also reported were the 95% confidence intervals (CI) [5.62, 8.31], 95% CI [−2.43, 4.31], and 95% CI [−4.29, −3.11), respectively.

APA CODE: 4.44

The four-subtest battery added to this prediction, $R^2 = .21$, $\Delta R^2 = .09$, $F(4, 144) = 3.56$, $p = .004$, 95% CI [.10, .32].

APA Code: 4.44

There was a significant relation between the task and the sex of the adult partner whom the children chose, $\chi^2(1, N = 58) = 14.78$, $p < .01$.

APA CODE: 4.44

For increasing drug dosages, the means were 5.6, 4.3, and 1.7, respectively.

APA CODE: 4.45

The students who agreed to participate ($N = 130$) were divided into groups according to the severity of their deficiency.

APA CODE: 4.45

One group of participants ($n = 34$) received tutorials in the use of the word processing program.

APA CODE: 4.45

The four-subtest battery added to this prediction, $R^2 = .21$, $\Delta R^2 = .09$, $F(4, 144) = 3.56$, $p = .004$, (95% CI = .10, .32).

APA CODE: 4.44

There was a significant relation between the task and the sex of the adult partner whom the children chose, $\chi^2_1(58) = 14.78$, $p < .01$.

APA CODE: 4.44

For increasing drug dosages, $Ms = 5.6$, 4.3, and 1.7, respectively.

APA CODE: 4.45

The students who agreed to participate ($n = 130$) were divided into groups according to the severity of their deficiency.

APA CODE: 4.45

One group of participants ($N = 34$) received tutorials in the use of the word processing program.

APA CODE: 4.45

Integrative Exercise: Statistical and Mathematical Copy

Results and Discussion

Figure 4 shows the mean phoneme boundaries for all conditions and the restoration effect for each captor type. The restoration effects are shown above the histogram bars both as a boundary shift in hertz and as a percentage of the difference in boundary position between the incremented-fourth and leading-fourth conditions. There was a highly significant effect of condition on the phoneme boundary values, $F(8, 88) = 53.16$, $p < .001$. Incrementing the level of the fourth harmonic lowered the phoneme boundary relative to the vowel-alone condition (by 51 Hz, $p < .001$), which indicates that the extra energy was integrated into the vowel percept. The leading-fourth condition led to a significantly higher phoneme boundary than did the incremented-fourth condition ($p < .001$) but did not differ from the vowel-alone condition ($p = .177$), showing that the extra energy was excluded from the vowel percept when it began 240 ms before the vowel. The phoneme boundaries for the captor-control conditions did not differ significantly from that for the incremented-fourth condition. These results are consistent with those found by Darwin and Sutherland (1984) and by Roberts and Holmes (2006).

Analysis of the restoration effects revealed that there was no significant difference between the three captor types, $F(2, 22) = 0.90$, $p = .421$. The overall size of the restoration effect (about 7.2 Hz, or 17%) was not quite significantly greater than 0, $t(11) = 2.01$, $p = .069$. However, an inspection of the individual data identified one listener who obtained negative restoration values for all three captor types, owing to an unusually small boundary return for the leading-fourth condition. For the other 11 listeners, the overall size of the restoration effect was significantly greater than 0, $t(10) = 3.34$, $p < .01$.

APA CODES: 4.41–4.51

Integrative Exercise: Statistical and Mathematical Copy

Results

Figure 4 shows the mean phoneme boundaries for all conditions and the restoration effect for each captor type. The restoration effects are shown above the histogram bars both as a boundary shift in Hz and as a percentage of the difference in boundary position between the incremented-fourth and leading-fourth conditions. There was a highly significant effect of condition on the phoneme boundary values, $F(8/88) = 53.16$, $p < 0.001$. Incrementing the level of the fourth harmonic lowered the phoneme boundary relative to the vowel-alone condition (by 51 Hz, p < .001), which indicates that the extra energy was integrated into the vowel percept. The leading-fourth condition led to a significantly higher phoneme boundary than did the incremented-fourth condition (p<.001) but did not differ from the vowel-alone condition (p=.177), showing that the extra energy was excluded from the vowel percept when it began 240 milliseconds before the vowel. The phoneme boundaries for the captor-control conditions did not differ significantly from that for the incremented-fourth condition. These results are consistent with those found by Darwin and Sutherland (1984) and by Roberts and Holmes (2006).

Analysis of the restoration effects revealed that there was no significant difference between the three captor types, $F = 0.90$, $df = 2, 22$, $p = 0.421$. The overall size of the restoration effect (about 7.2 Hz, or 17%) was not quite significantly greater than 0, $t = 2.01$, $df = 11$, $p = 0.069$. However, an inspection of the individual data identified one listener who obtained negative restoration values for all three captor types, owing to an unusually small boundary return for the leading-fourth condition. For the other 11 listeners, the overall size of the restoration effect was significantly greater than 0, $t = 3.34$, $df = 10$, $p < 0.01$.

APA CODES: 4.41–4.51

Tables
APA Codes: 5.01–5.19

NOTES:

Results

Table 1 shows the mean effectiveness ratings of the three types of therapists by the four evaluating groups. A 4 × 3 mixed analysis of variance indicated that the interaction between raters and therapy method was significant, $F(6, 152) = 19.6, p < .01$.

APA CODE: 5.03

■ *Note to students:* The feedback frame for this exercise is blank because Table 3 would not exist. The information would be provided more economically in the text of the paper.

Tables
APA Codes: 5.01–5.19

These exercises cover conciseness in tables, table layout, standard table forms, the relation of tables and text; the relation between tables, table numbers, table titles, table headings, the table body, confidence intervals in tables, table notes; the ruling of tables; presenting data in specific types of tables; and a table checklist (see the *Publication Manual*, sections 5.01–5.19). Mark corrections directly on the right-hand page, and compare your responses with the correct answers on the left-hand page. When you are finished with this section, take the research report practice test or take one of the research report mastery tests.

Results

The clinical trainers gave mean ratings of effectiveness to the directive, structured, and nondirective therapists of 4.7, 6.2, and 8.7, respectively; the working clinicians assigned ratings of 9.1, 5.3, and 3.6, respectively, to the same therapists; the clinical trainees gave mean ratings of 5.8, 6,6, and 6.4, respectively, to the three groups; and the client sample assigned ratings of 5.9, 3.8, and 1.4, respectively, to the three types of therapists. A 4×3 mixed analysis of variance indicated that the interaction between raters and therapy method was significant, $F(6, 152) = 19.6$, $p < .01$.

APA CODE: 5.03

Table 3

Mean Barking Duration (in Seconds) to Dinner Bell as a Function of Cat's Presence

Cat's presence	M
Absent	33
Present	5

APA CODE: 5.03

Results

As shown in Table 1, there were significant differences in U.S., $F(3, 88) = 4.63$, $p < .01$, but not community subjective social status, $F(3, 88) = 1.84$, $p > .05$, among women in different education groups.

APA CODE: 5.05

Table 2

Mean Time to Write Research Report After Different Kinds of Training and Prior Experience

No. prior reports	Type of training			
	None	Lecture	Mastery	Exercises
0	10.4	9.6	7.1	5.3
1	9.1	9.0	6.3	4.1
2	7.4	7.4	5.2	3.8

Note. Times are reported in hours. $n = 20$ in each condition.

■ ***Note to students:*** Other table titles would also suffice, as long as they are brief, identify the independent and dependent variables, and are not redundant with the headings in the table.

APA CODE: 5.12

Table 2

Efforts of Distance From Natural Disaster on Relevant Knowledge, Volunteerism, and Anxiety

APA CODE: 5.12

Results

As shown in table 1a, there were significant differences in U.S., $F(3, 88) = 4.63$, $p < .01$, but not community subjective social status, $F(3, 88) = 1.84$, $p > .05$, among women in different education groups.

APA CODE: 5.05

Table 2

A Table Listing the Mean Length of Time It Took Participants to Write a Research Report After They Received No Training, Lecture, Mastery Testing, or Exercises and Had Written Either 0, 1, or 2 Prior Reports

No. prior reports	Type of training			
	None	Lecture	Mastery	Exercises
0	10.4	9.6	7.1	5.3
1	9.1	9.0	6.3	4.1
2	7.4	7.4	5.2	3.8

Note. Times are reported in hours. $n = 20$ in each condition.

APA CODE: 5.12

Table 2: Effects of distance from natural disaster on relevant knowledge, volunteerism, and anxiety.

APA CODE: 5.12

Table 3

Individual and Family Characteristics as a Percentage of the Sample (Census Data in Parentheses)

Characteristic	Mother (n = 750)	Father (n = 466)	Child (n = 750)
Self-identity			
Mexican	77.2	71.0	41.0
Mexican American	22.8	29.0	59.0
Nativity[a]			
Mexico	74.2 (38.2)	80.0 (44.2)	29.7
United States	25.8 (61.8)	20.0 (55.8)	70.3
Language preference[b]			
English	30.2 (52.7)	23.2 (52.7)	82.5 (70.0)
Spanish	69.8 (48.3)	76.8 (48.3)	17.5 (30.0)
Education level completed[a]			
8th grade or less	29.2 (30.7)	30.2 (33.4)	
Some high school	19.5 (20.9)	22.4 (22.6)	
12th grade	23.1 (22.5)	20.9 (20.7)	
Some college/vocational training	22.0 (19.2)	20.2 (17.1)	
Bachelors or higher	6.2 (6.8)	6.2 (6.2)	
Employment status[c]			
Employed	63.6 (46.6)	96.6 (97.1)	
Unemployed	11.2 (3.5)	3.5 (2.9)	
Housewife	25.2		

Note. Adapted from "Sampling and Recruitment in Studies of Cultural Influences on Adjustment: A Case Study With Mexican Americans," by M. W. Roosa, F. F. Liu, M. Torres, N. A. Gonzales, G. P. Knight, and D. Saenz, 2008, *Journal of Family Psychology, 22,* p. 300. Copyright 2008 by the American Psychological Association.

[a]Census data are for all women or men and are not limited to parents or adults in our age group. [b]The most comparable census data for mothers and fathers are for all adults 18 years and older and for children are for 15- to 17-year-olds. [c]Census data are for all women, not just mothers, whereas the male data are limited to husbands.

APA CODE: 5.13

Table 3

Individual and Family Characteristics as a Percentage of the Sample (Census Data in Parentheses)

Individual and Family Characteristic	Mother (*n* = 750)	Father (*n* = 466)	Child (*n* = 750)
Mexican identity	77.2	71.0	41.0
Mexican American identity	22.8	29.0	59.0
Born in Mexico[a]	74.2 (38.2)	80.0 (44.2)	29.7
Born in United States[a]	25.8 (61.8)	20.0 (55.8)	70.3
English language preference[b]	30.2 (52.7)	23.2 (52.7)	82.5 (70.0)
Spanish language preference[b]	69.8 (48.3)	76.8 (48.3)	17.5 (30.0)
8th grade or less education completed[a]	29.2 (30.7)	30.2 (33.4)	
Some high school completed[a]	19.5 (20.9)	22.4 (22.6)	
12th grade completed[a]	23.1 (22.5)	20.9 (20.7)	
Some college/vocational training completed[a]	22.0 (19.2)	20.2 (17.1)	
Bachelors or higher completed[a]	6.2 (6.8)	6.2 (6.2)	
Employed status[c]	63.6 (46.6)	96.6 (97.1)	
Unemployed status[c]	11.2 (3.5)	3.5 (2.9)	
Housewife status[c]	25.2		

Note. Adapted from "Sampling and Recruitment in Studies of Cultural Influences on Adjustment: A Case Study With Mexican Americans," by M. W. Roosa, F. F. Liu, M. Torres, N. A. Gonzales, G. P. Knight, and D. Saenz, 2008, *Journal of Family Psychology, 22,* p. 300. Copyright 2008 by the American Psychological Association.

[a]Census data are for all women or men and are not limited to parents or adults in our age group. [b]The most comparable census data for mothers and fathers are for all adults 18 years and older and for children are for 15- to 17-year-olds. [c]Census data are for all women, not just mothers, whereas the male data are limited to husbands.

APA CODE: 5.13

Table 3

Aggression and Activity in Frogs as a Function of Food Scarcity and Musical Upbringing

	Food supply	
Musical heritage	Limited	Abundant
	Aggressive behavior[a]	
Rock and roll	3.8	0.8
Popular	3.4	0.4
Classical	3.6	1.2
	Activity level[b]	
Rock and roll	19.7	21.3
Popular	12.7	13.5
Classical	11.4	7.6

Note. $n = 16$ for all cells.

[a]Aggression was measured by number of bumps of another frog. [b]Activity level was measured by number of jumps.

Correct as is.

APA CODE: 5.13

Table 3

Aggression and Activity in Frogs as a Function of Food Scarcity and Musical Upbringing

Musical heritage	Food supply	
	Limited	Abundant
Aggressive behavior[a]		
Rock and roll	3.8	0.8
Popular	3.4	0.4
Classical	3.6	1.2
Activity level[b]		
Rock and roll	19.7	21.3
Popular	12.7	13.5
Classical	11.4	7.6

Note. $n = 16$ for all cells.

[a]Aggression was measured by number of bumps of another frog. [b]Activity level was measured by number of jumps.

APA CODE: 5.13

Table 6

Effects of Victim Reaction and Social Influence on Bystander Intervention

Setting	Victim screaming		
	Yes	No	*M*
Alone	23	17	20
Group	15	9	12
M	19	13	

■ **Note to students:** Certainly the row and column totals and means are redundant. Some authors would delete the totals. Others would not see a need to include the means either, because the means could be calculated easily by adding the columns or rows and dividing by two.

APA CODE: 5.14

Table 2

Summary of Intercorrelations, Means, and Standard Deviations for Scores on the BSS, BDI, SAFE, and MEIM as a Function of Race

Measure	1	2	3	4	*M*	*SD*
1. BSS	—	.54*	.29*	−.23*	1.31	4.32
2. BDI	.54*	—	.34*	−.14*	8.33	7.76
3. SAFE	.19*	.30*	—	−.074	47.18	13.24
4. MEIM	−.09	−.11	−.08	—	47.19	6.26
M	1.50	9.13	39.07	37.78		
SD	3.84	7.25	13.17	7.29		

Note. Intercorrelations for African American participants (*n* = 296) are presented above the diagonal, and intercorrelations for European American participants (*n* = 163) are presented below the diagonal. Means and standard deviations for African American students are presented in the vertical columns, and means and standard deviations for European Americans are presented in the horizontal rows. For all scales, higher scores are indicative of more extreme responding in the direction of the construct assessed. BSS = Beck Suicide Scale; BDI = Beck Depression Inventory; SAFE = Social, Attitudinal, Familial, and Environmental Acculturation Stress Scale; MEIM = Multigroup Ethnic Identity Measure. Adapted from "An Empirical Investigation of Stress and Ethnic Identity as Moderators for Depression and Suicidal Ideation in College Students," by R. L. Walker, L. R. Wingate, E. M. Obasi, and T. E. Joiner, 2008, *Cultural Diversity and Ethnic Minority Psychology, 14,* p. 78. Copyright 2008 by the American Psychological Association.
*$p < .01$.

Correct as is.

APA CODE: 5.14

Table 6

Effects of Victim Reaction and Social Influence on Bystander Intervention

| Setting | Victim screaming | | Total | *M* |
	Yes	No		
Alone	23	17	40	20
Group	15	9	24	12
Total	38	26		
M	19	13		

APA CODE: 5.14

Table 2

Summary of Intercorrelations, Means and Standard Deviations for Scores on the BSS, BDI, SAFE, and MEIM as a Function of Race

Measure	1	2	3	4	*M*	*SD*
1. BSS	—	.54*	.29*	−.23*	1.31	4.32
2. BDI	.54*	—	.34*	−.14*	8.33	7.76
3. SAFE	.19*	.30*	—	−.074	47.18	13.24
4. MEIM	−.09	−.11	−.08	—	47.19	6.26
M	1.50	9.13	39.07	37.78		
SD	3.84	7.25	13.17	7.29		

Note. Intercorrelations for African American participants ($n = 296$) are presented above the diagonal, and intercorrelations for European American participants ($n = 163$) are presented below the diagonal. Means and standard deviations for African American students are presented in the vertical columns, and means and standard deviations for European Americans are presented in the horizontal rows. For all scales, higher scores are indicative of more extreme responding in the direction of the construct assessed. BSS = Beck Suicide Scale; BDI = Beck Depression Inventory; SAFE = Social, Attitudinal, Familial, and Environmental Acculturation Stress Scale; MEIM = Multigroup Ethnic Identity Measure. Adapted from "An Empirical Investigation of Stress and Ethnic Identity as Moderators for Depression and Suicidal Ideation in College Students," by R. L. Walker, L. R. Wingate, E. M. Obasi, and T. E. Joiner, 2008, *Cultural Diversity and Ethnic Minority Psychology, 14,* p. 78. Copyright 2008 by the American Psychological Association.
*$p < .01$.

APA CODE: 5.16

Table 1

Number of Textbook Pages Read for Different Academic Participants in Different Locations

Subject	Study location			
	Dorm	Outdoors	Lounge	Library
Education	4.6	0.8	3.0	6.2
Humanities	9.8	14.1	6.6	33.5
Mathematics	14.2	1.4	3.1	18.4
Science	22.4	3.1	11.0	18.1

Note. Scores are mean number of pages completed. $n = 20$ per cell.

APA CODE: 5.14

Table 4

Weight Status, Body Dissatisfaction, and Weight Control Behaviors at Time 1 and Suicidal Ideation at Time 2

Variable	Unadjusted[a]		Adjusted for demographic variables[b]	
	OR	95% CI	OR	95% CI
Weight status				
Young men	0.97	[0.78, 1.21]	0.94	[0.75, 1.19]
Young women	1.06	[0.88, 1.26]	1.02	[0.85, 1.23]
Body dissatisfaction				
Young men	0.88	[0.50, 1.54]	0.99	[0.56, 1.75]
Young women	1.06	[0.77, 1.46]	1.02	[0.74, 1.42]
UWCB				
Young men	0.81	[0.54, 1.24]	0.77	[0.50, 1.19]
Young women	0.89	[0.65, 1.21]	0.93	[0.68, 1.27]
EWCB				
Young men	1.36	[0.55, 3.36]	1.73	[0.69, 4.37]
Young women	1.98	[1.34, 2.93]	2.00	[1.34, 2.99]

Note. OR = odds ratio; CI = confidence interval; UWCB = healthy weight control behaviors; EWCB = extreme weight control behaviors. Adapted from "Are Body Dissatisfaction, Eating Disturbance, and Body Mass Index Predictors of Suicidal Behavior in Adolescents? A Longitudinal Study," by S. Crow, M. E. Eisenberg, M. Story, and D. Neumark-Sztainer, 2008, *Journal of Consulting and Clinical Psychology, 76*, p. 890. Copyright 2008 by the American Psychological Association. [a]Four weight-related variables entered simultaneously. [b]Adjusted for race, socioeconomic status, and age group.

APA CODES: 5.15–5.16

Table 1

Number of Textbook Pages Read for Different Academic Participants in Different Locations

Subject	Study location			
	Dorm	Outdoors	Lounge	Library
Education	4.6	0.75	3.0	6.2
Humanities	9.8	14.1	6.6	33.50
Mathematics	14.2	1.414	3.1416	18.40
Science	22.4	3.14	11.00	18.12

Note. Scores are mean number of pages completed. $n = 20$ per cell.

APA CODE: 5.14

Table 4

Weight Status, Body Dissatisfaction, and Weight Control Behaviors at Time 1 and Suicidal Ideation at Time 2

Variable	Unadjusted[1]		Adjusted for demographic variables[2]	
	OR	95% CI	OR	95% CI
Weight status				
Young men	0.97	0.78, 1.21	0.94	0.75, 1.19
Young women	1.06	0.88, 1.26	1.02	0.85, 1.23
Body dissatisfaction				
Young men	0.88	0.50, 1.54	0.99	0.56, 1.75
Young women	1.06	0.77, 1.46	1.02	0.74, 1.42
UWCB				
Young men	0.81	0.54, 1.24	0.77	0.50, 1.19
Young women	0.89	0.65, 1.21	0.93	0.68, 1.27
EWCB				
Young men	1.36	0.55, 3.36	1.73	0.69, 4.37
Young women	1.98	1.34, 2.93	2.00	1.34, 2.99

Note. OR = odds ratio; CI = confidence interval; UWCB = unhealthy weight control behaviors; EWCB = extreme weight control behaviors. Adapted from "Are Body Dissatisfaction, Eating Disturbance, and Body Mass Index Predictors of Suicidal Behavior in Adolescents? A Longitudinal Study," by S. Crow, M. E. Eisenberg, M. Story, and D. Neumark-Sztainer, 2008, *Journal of Consulting and Clinical Psychology, 76,* p. 890. Copyright 2008 by the American Psychological Association.
[1]Four weight-related variables entered simultaneously. [2]Adjusted for race, socioeconomic status, and age group.

APA CODES: 5.15–5.16

Table X

Predictors of Self-Reported Moral Behavior

Variable	Model 1 B	Model 2 B	95% CI
Constant	3.192**	2.99	[2.37, 3.62]
Gender	0.18*	0.17	[−0.00, 0.33]
Age	−0.06	−0.05	[−0.14, 0.03]
Social desirability bias	−0.08**	−0.08**	[−0.10, −0.05]
Moral identity internalization	−0.17**	−0.16**	[−0.26, −0.06]
Moral identity symbolization	0.07*	0.06	[−0.01, 0.12]
Perceptual moral attentiveness		0.07*	[0.00, 0.13]
Reflective moral attentiveness		−0.01	[−0.08, 0.06]
R^2	.29	.31	
F	19.07**	14.46**	
ΔR^2		.01	
ΔF		2.39	

Note. $N = 242$. CI = confidence interval. Adapted from "Moral Attentiveness: Who Pays Attention to the Moral Aspects of Life?" by S. J. Reynolds, 2008, *Journal of Applied Psychology, 93,* p. 1035. Copyright 2008 by the American Psychological Association.
*$p < .05$. **$p < .01$.

APA CODES: 5.15–5.16

Table X

Predictors of Self-Reported Moral Behavior

| Variable | Self-reported moral behavior | | |
| | Model 1 B | Model 2 | |
		B	95% CI
Constant	3.192**	2.99	[2.37, 3.62]
Gender	0.18*	0.17	[−0.00, 0.33]
Age	−0.06	−0.05	[−0.14, 0.03]
Social desirability bias	−0.08**	−0.08**	[−0.10, −0.05]
Moral identity internalization	−0.17**	−0.16**	[−0.26, −0.06]
Moral identity symbolization	0.07*	0.06	[−0.01, 0.12]
Perceptual moral attentiveness		0.07*	[0.00, 0.13]
Reflective moral attentiveness		−0.01	[−0.08, 0.06]
R^2	.29	.31	
F	19.07**	14.46**	
ΔR^2		.01	
ΔF		2.39	

Note. Sample size = 242. Adapted from "Moral Attentiveness: Who Pays Attention to the Moral Aspects of Life?" by S. J. Reynolds, 2008, *Journal of Applied Psychology, 93,* p. 1035. Copyright 2008 by the American Psychological Association.

Two asterisks indicate $p < .01$. One asterisk indicates $p < .05$.

APA CODES: 5.15–5.16

Table X

Psychometric Properties of the Major Study Variables

Variable	n	M	SD	α	Range Potential	Range Actual	Skew
Dispositional affectivity							
Positive	560	3.27	0.77	.91	1–5	1.0–5.0	−0.36
Negative	563	2.26	0.79	.91	1–5	1.0–4.7	0.63
Social support							
Mother	160	4.17	1.08	.92	1–5	1.0–5.0	−1.54
Partner	474	4.03	1.19	.94	1–5	1.0–5.0	−1.26
Friend	396	4.37	0.89	.90	1–5	1.0–5.0	−1.94
Social conflict							
Mother	159	1.22	0.47	.81	1–5	1.0–3.6	3.07
Partner	471	1.40	0.79	.90	1–5	1.0–5.0	2.63
Friend	381	1.15	0.45	.79	1–5	1.0–5.0	5.27
Postabortion adjustment							
Distress	609	0.59	0.63	.90	0–4	0.0–3.0	1.56
Well-being	606	4.60	0.69	.85	1–6	2.3–6.0	−0.53

Note. The variation in sample size is due to the variation in the number of women who told a particular source about the abortion. From "Mixed Messages: Implications of Social Conflict and Social Support Within Close Relationships for Adjustment to a Stressful Life Event," by B. Major, J. M. Zubek, M. L. Cooper, C. Cozzarelli, and C. Richards, 1997, *Journal of Personality and Social Psychology*, p. 1355. Copyright 1997 by the American Psychological Association.

Correct as is.

APA CODE: 5.18

Table X

Psychometric Properties of the Major Study Variables

Variable	n	M	SD	α	Range Potential	Actual	Skew
Dispositional affectivity							
Positive	560	3.27	0.77	.91	1–5	1.0–5.0	−0.36
Negative	563	2.26	0.79	.91	1–5	1.0–4.7	0.63
Social support							
Mother	160	4.17	1.08	.92	1–5	1.0–5.0	−1.54
Partner	474	4.03	1.19	.94	1–5	1.0–5.0	−1.26
Friend	396	4.37	0.89	.90	1–5	1.0–5.0	−1.94
Social conflict							
Mother	159	1.22	0.47	.81	1–5	1.0–3.6	3.07
Partner	471	1.40	0.79	.90	1–5	1.0–5.0	2.63
Friend	381	1.15	0.45	.79	1–5	1.0–5.0	5.27
Postabortion adjustment							
Distress	609	0.59	0.63	.90	0–4	0.0–3.0	1.56
Well-being	606	4.60	0.69	.85	1–6	2.3–6.0	−0.53

Note. The variation in sample size is due to the variation in the number of women who told a particular source about the abortion. From "Mixed Messages: Implications of Social Conflict and Social Support Within Close Relationships for Adjustment to a Stressful Life Event," by B. Major, J. M. Zubek, M. L. Cooper, C. Cozzarelli, and C. Richards, 1997, *Journal of Personality and Social Psychology,* p. 1355. Copyright 1997 by the American Psychological Association.

APA CODE: 5.18

Integrative Exercise: Tables

Table 1

Distribution of Eyewitness Errors During Different Kinds of Interviews After an Actual Murder

Error type	Interviewer	
	Police[a]	Researcher[b]
Actions	53.3	48.5
Descriptions		
People	41.1	34.3
Objects	5.6	17.2

Note. Scores represent the percentage of errors of each type combined over the 11 eyewitnesses. Each eyewitness could make more than one error of each particular type.
[a]Total errors = 107. [b]Total errors = 198.

■ ***Note to students:*** Other brief titles that specify the independent and dependent variables nonredundantly would also be correct. Furthermore, the arrangement of the table shown above is not the only correct presentation. Depending on the perspective you take in the text, you could have the two different interviewers arranged in the rows and the three different error types arranged in the columns.

APA CODES: 5.07–5.19

Integrative Exercise: Tables

Table 1 *Distribution of Eyewitness Errors About Actions, Descriptions of People, and Descriptions of Objects During Interviews by Police and Researchers After an Actual Murder.*

Error Type	Interviewer
	Police[a]
action descriptions	53.271
People	41.121
Objects	5.607
	Researcher[b]
action descriptions	48.485
People	34.343
Objects	17.172

Note. Scores represent the percentage of errors of each type combined over the 11 eyewitnesses. Each eyewitness could make more than one error of each particular type. Footnote[a]. Total errors = 107. Footnote[b]. Total errors = 198.

APA CODES: 5.07–5.19

Research Report Practice Test

The practice test, formatted like the familiarization test, is designed to assess your level of mastery after completing the learning and integrative exercises and help you to decide whether (a) to study particular topics in the *Publication Manual* in more depth, (b) to go on to the review exercises, or (d) to take a mastery test. Take this 41-question multiple-choice test. There are two answer sheets at the end of the test, one blank for you to write in your answers and the other containing the correct answers. Beside each blank you will find the APA code that corresponds to the *Publication Manual* section containing the relevant style rule and example. Score your test using the answer key with the correct answers. If you score low (i.e., 80% or lower) on the practice test, we advise you to do the review exercises at the end of the research report unit. If you score above 80%, you may want to take a mastery test, which your instructor will supply.

RESEARCH REPORT PRACTICE TEST

1. A report of an empirical study usually includes an introduction and sections called Method, Results, and

   a. Statistics.
   b. Bibliography.
   c. Discussion.
   d. Statement of the Problem.

2. The abstract of an article should

   a. report rather than evaluate.
   b. be a brief, comprehensive summary of the contents of the article.
   c. be dense with information.
   d. do all of the above.

3. What question should the introduction section of a research report attempt to answer?

   a. What are the theoretical implications of the current research?
   b. Why is this problem important?
   c. What is the logical link between the problem and the research design?
   d. All of the above are correct.
   e. Only a and c of the above are correct.

4. The Method section should

   a. include enough detail to make replication of the experiment possible for the reader.
   b. briefly describe the method to the reader, omitting details about subjects and apparatus.
   c. fully describe all statistical testing procedures used.
   d. explain why the study was done.

5. The Results section should include

   a. dates defining the periods of recruitment and follow up and primary sources of the potential subjects.
   b. adverse events and/or side effects, if interventions were studied.
   c. baseline demographic and/or clinical characteristics of each group.
   d. research design.
   e. all of the above except d

6. In reporting your data

    a. do not mention results that run counter to expectation.

    b. include all individual scores and raw data.

    c. do not discuss implications of the results.

    d. do not assume your reader has a professional knowledge of statistical methods.

7. A sufficient set of statistics usually includes

    a. cell standard deviations.

    b. observed cell means.

    c. per-cell sample sizes.

    d. all of the above.

8. Edit the following by selecting the correct arrangement of headings:

Method

Subjects

Procedure

Results

Discussion

    a. leave as is

    b.

Method

Subjects

Procedure

Results

Discussion

    c.

Method

Subjects

Procedure

Results

Discussion

    d.

Method

Subjects

Procedure

Results

Discussion

9. What causes the following segment of a student's research report to lack smoothness of expression?

   According to the research of Savin-Williams (1988), how gay men publicly revealed their sexual orientation is correlated with the stability of their mental health. He finds that well-adjusted gay men reveal early to trusted others.

   a. intransitive inferences
   b. too much jargon
   c. abrupt changes in verb tense
   d. misplaced modifiers

10. Speculation is in order in the Discussion section when it is

    a. identified as speculation.
    b. logically related to empirical data or the theory being tested.
    c. expressed concisely.
    d. all of the above.
    e. none of the above.

11. When a verb concerns the action of the author–experimenter, the

    a. third person and passive voice should be used.
    b. third person and active voice should be used.
    c. the first person, active voice should be used.
    d. third person should be used in all scientific writing to ensure objectivity.

12. Which of the following examples demonstrates correct use of capitalization?

    a. Trial 3 and Item 4
    b. trial *n* and item *x*
    c. Chapter 4
    d. Table 2 and Figure 3
    e. All of the above are correct.

13. Edit the following for capitalization:

    When the hermit crabs listened to classical music, they were significantly more likely to retreat back into their shells than when they listened to rock-and-roll music. However, there was no music x shell interaction effect.

    a. leave as is
    b. The interaction term *music x* shell should *be Music x* Shell.
    c. Statistical terms such as *significantly* should be capitalized.
    d. *Interaction effect* should be *Interaction Effect*.

14. According to the APA style rules regarding italics,

    a. only Greek letters used as statistical symbols are italicized.
    b. all letters used as statistical symbols except Greek letters should be italicized.
    c. letters used as statistical symbols are never italicized in print.
    d. a and c of the above are correct.

15. Numerals should be used at all times for

    a. numbers in the abstract of a paper or in a graphical display within a paper.
    b. ratios, arithmetical manipulations, and series of four or more numbers.
    c. fractional or decimal quantities, scores and points on a scale, and units of measurement of time.
    d. all of the above.

16. Edit the following for the expression of numbers:

    It would be wrong to estimate absentees for the week by taking the number of absentees on Monday and multiplying by 5.

    a. leave as is
    b. It would be wrong to estimate absentees for the week by taking the number of absentees on Monday and multiplying by five.
    c. It would be wrong to estimate absentees for the week by taking the number of absentees on Monday and multiplying by five (5).

17. Edit the following for the expression of numbers:

    The authors identified 7 different groups of personality theories.

    a. leave as is
    b. The authors identified seven different groups of personality theories.
    c. The authors identified seven (7) different groups of personality theories.

18. Edit the following for the expression of numbers:

    Large financial responsibility was defined as responsibility for an annual budget in excess of five million dollars.

    a. leave as is
    b. *Large* financial responsibility was defined as responsibility for an annual budget in excess of 5×10^6.
    c. *Large* financial responsibility was defined as responsibility for an annual budget in excess of $5,000,000.
    d. *Large* financial responsibility was defined as responsibility for an annual budget in excess of $5 million.

19. Edit the following for the expression of ordinal numbers:

The students were all in their second year of graduate school.

    a. leave as is

    b. The students were all in their second (2nd) year of graduate school.

    c. The students were all in their 2nd year of graduate school.

20. When using numbers less than one,

    a. a zero is always used before the decimal point (0.05).

    b. a zero is never used before the decimal point (.05).

    c. the author should check with the editor of each specific journal, as this is a highly controversial topic.

    d. a zero is used before the decimal point (0.05) except when the number cannot be greater than 1 (e.g., correlations, proportions, and levels of statistical significance; $r(24) = -.43$, $p = .028$).

21. Edit the following for the expression of numbers:

Days I and IV were baseline days, and Days II and III were treatment days.

    a. leave as is

    b. Days One and Four were baseline days, and Days Two and Three were treatment days.

    c. Days 1 and 4 were baseline days, and Days 2 and 3 were treatment days.

    d. Days I and Four were baseline days, and Days II and III were treatment days.

22. Which example is the correct way to use commas and spacing when presenting statistics in text?

    a. $F_{,}(24, 1000)$

    b. $F(24, 1{,}000)$

    c. $F(24, 1000)$

    d. $F(24\ 1{,}000)$

23. Which of the following metric units is correctly expressed?

    a. 33 cms.

    b. 3 mm.

    c. 13 cm

    d. 3 cms.

24. Edit the following for the citation of a statistic in text:

A 4 × 3 analysis of variance (Woodworth, 2005) was conducted on the preference scores.

   a. leave as is
   b. A 4 × 3 analysis of variance (see any standard statistics text) was conducted on the preference scores.
   c. A 4 × 3 analysis of variance was conducted on the preference scores.

25. Edit the following for the presentation of formulas:

The relation between premarital sexual experience and incidence of divorce was evaluated using a chi-square test $\{\chi^2 = [\Sigma(\text{Observed} - \text{Expected})/\text{Expected}]\}$.

   a. leave as is
   b. The relationship between premarital sexual experience and incidence of divorce was evaluated using a chi-square test (see Appendix A for formula).
   c. The relationship between premarital sexual experience and incidence of divorce was evaluated using a chi-square test.

26. When presenting statistical information in the text, to clarify the nature of effects (i.e., mean differences and the direction of mean differences),

   a. give only the inferential statistics.
   b. always give descriptive and inferential statistics.
   c. give inferential and descriptive statistics only when presenting correlational data.
   d. give inferential statistics for experiments with more than one independent variable and descriptive statistics for correlational research.

27. When reporting confidence intervals,

   a. use the format 95% CI [LL, UL], where LL is the lower limit of the confidence interval and UL is the upper limit.
   b. always report the level of confidence.
   c. do not repeat 95% CI when a sequence of confidence intervals are repeated in a series if the level remains unchanged and the meaning is clear.
   d. all of the above.

28. Edit the following for the use of statistical symbols:

    In the group therapy condition, 16 percent of the clients did not return for the second session and another 8 percent did not return for the third session.

    a. leave as is

    b. In the group therapy condition, 16% of the clients did not return for the second session and another eight percent did not return for the third session.

    c. In the group therapy condition, 16% of the clients did not return for the second session and another eight % did not return for the third session.

    d. In the group therapy condition, 16% of the clients did not return for the second session and another 8% did not return for the third session.

29. Edit the following for typing statistical and mathematical copy:

    High-school GPA statistically predicted college mathematics performance, $R^2 = .12$, $F(1, 148) = 20.18$, $p < .001$, 95% CI (.02, .22). The four-subtest battery added to this prediction, $R^2 = .21$, $\Delta R^2 = .09$, $F(4, 144) = 3.56$, $p = .004$, 95% CI (.10, .32). Most important, when the two preceding variables were statistically accounted for, the college mathematics placement examination also explained unique variance in students' college mathematics performance, $R^2 = .25$, $\Delta R^2 = .04$, $F(1, 143) = 7.63$, $p = .006$, 95% CI (.13, .37).

    a. leave as is

    b. High-school GPA statistically predicted college mathematics performance, $R^2 = .12$, $F(1, 148) = 20.18$, $p< .001$, 95% CI [.02, .22]. The four-subtest battery added to this prediction, $R^2 = .21$, $\Delta R^2 = .09$, $F(4, 144) = 3.56$, $p= .004$, 95% CI [.10, .32]. Most important, when the two preceding variables were statistically accounted for, the college mathematics placement examination also explained unique variance in students' college mathematics performance, $R^2 = .25$, $\Delta R^2 = .04$, $F(1, 143) = 7.63$, $p= .006$, 95% CI [.13, .37].

    c. High-school GPA statistically predicted college mathematics performance, $R^2 = .12$, $F(1,148) = 20.18$, $p < .001$, 95% CI [.02, .22]. The four-subtest battery added to this prediction, $R^2 = .21$, $\Delta R^2 = .09$, $F(4,144) = 3.56$, $p= .004$, 95% CI [.10, .32]. Most important, when the two preceding variables were statistically accounted for, the college mathematics placement examination also explained unique variance in students' college mathematics performance, $R^2 = .25$, $\Delta R^2 = .04$, $F(1,143) = 7.63$, $p = .006$, 95% CI [.13, .37].

    d. High-school GPA statistically predicted college mathematics performance, $R^2 = .12$, $F(1, 148) = 20.18$, $p < .001$, 95% CI [.02, .22]. The four-subtest battery added to this prediction, $R^2 = .21$, $\Delta R^2 = .09$, $F(4, 144) = 3.56$, $p = .004$, 95% CI [.10, .32]. Most important, when the two preceding variables were statistically accounted for, the college mathematics placement examination also explained unique variance in students' college mathematics performance, $R^2 = .25$, $\Delta R^2 = .04$, $F(1, 143) = 7.63$, $p = .006$, 95% CI [.13, .37].

30. Which of the following should be used to designate the number of cases or observations in a total sample?

   a. *N*

   b. N

   c. *n*

   d. n

31. Edit the following for numbering of figures. Assume that this is the first time the figures are presented.

   Results

   The predicted social facilitation effects were observed. As can be seen in Figure 2, a video-camera increased errors with the difficult task and decreased errors with the easy task. As can be seen in Figure 1, the presence of an evaluative audience produced the same pattern of results.

   a. leave as is

   b. Figure 2 should be Figure II.

   c. Figure 2 should be Figure Two.

   d. Figure 2 should be Figure 1 and vice versa.

32. Edit Table 17 for errors in tabular presentation and notes to a table:

Table 17

Mean Mood Scores Before and After Physical Activity

Physical activity	Mood	
	Before	After
Nonaerobic		
Bird watching	3.2	3.7
Bowling	3.0	3.0
Golfing[a]	3.4	2.7
Aerobic		
Cycling	3.3	8.1
Dancing[b]	3.3	8.4
Hill climbing	3.2	8.2
Rowing	3.1	8.0
Running	3.4	7.9
Skiing/skating	3.1	9.0

Note. Mood was rated on a 10-point scale.

[a]Golfers rode around the course in golf carts. [b]Dancers danced to rock-and-roll music.

a. The mean values are rounded off too much.

b. There is not enough spacing between columns.

c. The footnotes are in the wrong sequence.

d. Roman numerals should be used to number a table.

e. There are no errors in Table 17.

33. Of the following possible titles for Table 17 (see Question 28), which would not be clear and explanatory?

a. *Mood and Exercise*

b. *Mean Changes in Mood of Subjects Prior to and Following a Variety of Nonaerobic and Aerobic Physical Activities*

c. *A Comparison of Physical Activities*

d. All of the above titles are poorly written.

34. Identify a column spanner in Table 17 (see Question 32):

a. Bird watching

b. Cycling

c. Mood

d. Aerobic

35. In Table 17 (see Question 32), identify a column heading:

a. Nonaerobic

b. Skiing/skating

c. Before

d. Mood

36. A specific note to a table

a. refers to a particular column or individual entry,

b. is indicated by a superscript lowercase letter.

c. is placed below the table.

d. does all of the above.

e. does none of the above.

37. Tables, including titles and headings, should be

a. triple-spaced.

b. double-spaced or single-spaced.

c. single-spaced.

d. any of the above.

38. A good figure

    a. conveys only essential facts.
    b. is easy to understand.
    c. is prepared in the same style as similar figures in the same article.
    d. does all of the above.

39. When presenting electrophysiological or event-related brain potential data, it is essential to include

    a. clear labeling.
    b. direction of negativity.
    c. scale of the response.
    d. all of the above.

40. Where should figures be placed in a submitted manuscript?

    a. at the end
    b. at the beginning
    c. in an appropriate place in text
    d. None of the above is correct.

41. A running head to be used in a research report should be typed

    a. centered at the bottom of the title page in all uppercase letters.
    b. flush left at the top of the title page.
    c. centered at the bottom of the title page in uppercase and lowercase letters.
    d. flush right at the bottom of the title page.

RESEARCH REPORT PRACTICE TEST
ANSWER SHEET AND FEEDBACK REPORT

Student Name _____ **Date** _____

Question Number	Answer	APA Codes	Question Number	Answer	APA Codes
1	_____	1.01–1.06	22	_____	4.31–4.38
2	_____	2.04	23	_____	4.39–4.40
3	_____	2.05–2.06	24	_____	4.41–4.48
4	_____	2.05–2.06	25	_____	4.41–4.48
5	_____	2.06–2.07	26	_____	4.41–4.48
6	_____	2.07–2.11	27	_____	4.41–4.48
7	_____	2.07–2.11	28	_____	4.41–4.48
8	_____	3.02–3.03	29	_____	4.41–4.48
9	_____	3.05–3.06	30	_____	4.41–4.48
10	_____	3.05–3.06	31	_____	5.05
11	_____	3.09	32	_____	5.07–5.19
12	_____	4.14–4.20	33	_____	5.07–5.19
13	_____	4.14–4.20	34	_____	5.07–5.19
14	_____	4.21	35	_____	5.07–5.19
15	_____	4.31–4.38	36	_____	5.07–5.19
16	_____	4.31–4.38	37	_____	5.17–5.19
17	_____	4.31–4.38	38	_____	5.20–5.28
18	_____	4.31–4.38	39	_____	5.20–5.28
19	_____	4.31–4.38	40	_____	8.03
20	_____	4.31–4.38	41	_____	8.03
21	_____	4.31–4.38			

NUMBER CORRECT _____

RESEARCH REPORT PRACTICE TEST
ANSWER KEY

Question Number	Answer	APA Codes	Question Number	Answer	APA Codes
1	c	1.01–1.06	22	c	4.31–4.38
2	d	2.04	23	c	4.39–4.40
3	d	2.05–2.06	24	c	4.41–4.48
4	a	2.05–2.06	25	c	4.41–4.48
5	e	2.06–2.07	26	b	4.41–4.48
6	c	2.07–2.11	27	d	4.41–4.48
7	d	2.07–2.11	28	d	4.41–4.48
8	b	3.02–3.03	29	d	4.41–4.48
9	c	3.05–3.06	30	a	4.41–4.48
10	c	3.05–3.06	31	d	5.05
11	c	3.09	32	e	5.07–5.19
12	e	4.14–4.20	33	d	5.07–5.19
13	b	4.14–4.20	34	c	5.07–5.19
14	b	4.21	35	c	5.07–5.19
15	d	4.31–4.38	36	d	5.07–5.19
16	a	4.31–4.38	37	b	5.17–5.19
17	b	4.31–4.38	38	d	5.20–5.28
18	d	4.31–4.38	39	d	5.20–5.28
19	c	4.31–4.38	40	a	8.03
20	d	4.31–4.38	41	b	8.03
21	c	4.31–4.38			

Research Report Review Exercises

Review exercises are all in the integrative format and cover the same topics as the learning exercises and integrative exercises. The components in need of correction are not shaded, but the errors in each review exercise are all related to the style rules contained in a specific part of the *Publication Manual* (e.g., tables, metrication). Read the text carefully and edit the text, marking corrections directly on the draft version. The corrections on the feedback page are shaded. Review exercises are designed to give you additional practice, to help you review style points you have already studied, and to further prepare you to take a mastery test.

Review Exercise: Headings and Series

Method

Participants

The participants were 228 students from an introductory psychology course who volunteered to attend an extra lecture of the course.

Design

The investigation included two predictor variables and one manipulated variable. One predictor variable, sex of the student, was dichotomous; the other predictor variable, student's score on Exam 1 of the course, was treated as a continuous variable. The manipulated variable was method of delivery of the lecture.

Procedure

Recruitment of participants. During the second unit of the course, which followed Exam 1, the major topic was learning and behavior control. The students were invited to attend an extra lecture, outside of the regularly scheduled class time. The instructor told the students that (a) they could sign up for any of a variety of times, (b) the lecture would be presented on videotape, (c) the lecture would describe applications of behavior-modification techniques to clinical and personal problems, (d) the material was optional and would not be tested directly on the next exam, and (e) the discussion of the applications would probably help the students understand the basic principles that would be covered on the next exam.

Manipulation of lecture delivery. Three videotapes were made of the instructor delivering the identical lecture: (a) reading, for which the instructor kept her head down to read the entire lecture, making eye contact with the camera only rarely; (b) using notes, for which the instructor glanced down frequently but also made occasional eye contact with the camera; and (c) from memory, for which the instructor had no notes and made frequent eye contact with the camera. The instructor was dressed the same and said the identical words on all three tapes. Students viewed the videotapes in groups of four to eight students each. Tapes were assigned to groups randomly, with an attempt to equalize the number of students who received each form of delivery.

Predictor variables. At the end of the videotape, the purpose of the investigation was explained to the students. They were each given a card on which to record their sex and their score on Exam 1 (a list of students and exam scores was available for the students to check their own scores).

Dependent measures. The experimenter, who showed the videotape, then recorded on each student's card the number of lines on which the student had written notes (as the measure of amount of notes) and the number of indentation shifts in the student's notes (as the measure of organization of notes).

Results

Review Exercise: Headings and Series

Method

Participants

The participants were 228 students from an introductory psychology course who volunteered to attend an extra lecture of the course.

Design

The investigation included two predictor variables and one manipulated variable. One predictor variable, sex of the student, was dichotomous; the other predictor variable, student's score on Exam 1 of the course, was treated as a continuous variable. The manipulated variable was method of delivery of the lecture.

Procedure

Recruitment of participant. During the second unit of the course, which followed Exam 1, the major topic was learning and behavior control. The students were invited to attend an extra lecture, outside of the regularly scheduled class time. The instructor told the students that a: they could sign up for any of a variety of times, b: the lecture would be presented on videotape, c: the lecture would describe applications of behavior-modification techniques to clinical and personal problems, d: the material was optional and would not be tested directly on the next exam, and e: the discussion of the applications would probably help the students understand the basic principles that would be covered on the next exam.

Manipulation of lecture delivery. Three videotapes were made of the instructor delivering the identical lecture: (1) reading, for which the instructor kept her head down to read the entire lecture, making eye contact with the camera only rarely (2) using notes, for which the instructor glanced down frequently but also made occasional eye contact with the camera, and (3) from memory, for which the instructor had no notes and made frequent eye contact with the camera. The instructor was dressed the same and said the identical words on all three tapes. Students viewed the videotapes in groups of four to eight students each. Tapes were assigned to groups randomly with an attempt to equalize the number of students who received each form of delivery.

Predictor variables. At the end of the videotape, the purpose of the investigation was explained to the students. They were each given a card on which to record their sex and their score on Exam 1 (a list of students and exam scores was available for the students to check their own scores).

Dependent measures. The experimenter, who showed the videotape, then recorded on each student's card the number of lines on which the student had written notes (as the measure of amount of notes) and the number of indentation shifts in the student's notes (as the measure of organization of notes).

Results

APA CODES: 3.02–3.04

Review Exercise: Capitalization

In their article "Work That Works Groups: Performance Enhancement With Disjunctive Tasks," Blaine and Walker (1989) concluded that groups can appear to do better than individuals when tasks allow disjunctive problem-solving processes. However, with conjunctive tasks, individuals appear to perform better than groups. Because there was a Group Size x Task interaction, selection of only one task yielded results that favored either social loafing theory or assembly bonus theory.

To test their hypothesis, we compared the performance of individuals assigned to either a conjunctive task condition or a disjunctive task condition. The expected results of Trials 1, 2, and 3 are displayed in Figure 1.

APA CODES: 4.14–4.20

Review Exercise: Capitalization

In their article "Work that works groups: Performance enhancement with disjunctive tasks," Blaine and Walker (1989) concluded that groups can appear to do better than individuals when tasks allow disjunctive problem-solving processes. However, with Conjunctive Tasks, individuals appear to perform better than groups. Because there was a group size X task interaction, selection of only one task yielded results that favored either Social Loafing theory or Assembly Bonus Theory.

To test their hypothesis, we compared the performance of individuals assigned to either a Conjunctive Task Condition or a Disjunctive Task Condition. The expected results of trials 1, 2, and 3 are displayed in figure 1.

APA CODES: 4.14–4.20

Review Exercise: Abbreviations

Analyses focus on participants' reaction times (RTs) to the 120 trials in which a target was present and was from a different emotional category from the distractor (e.g., RTs were not included for arrays containing eight images of a cat and one image of a butterfly because cats and butterflies are both positive low arousal items). Reaction times were analyzed for 24 trials of each target emotion category. Reaction times for error trials were excluded (fewer than 5% of all responses) as were RTs that were ±3 *SD* from each participant's mean (approximately 1.5% of responses). Median RTs were then calculated for each of the five emotional target categories, collapsing across array type (see Table 2 for raw RT values for each of the two age groups). This allowed us to examine, for example, whether participants were faster to detect images of snakes than images of mushrooms, regardless of the type of array in which they were presented. Because our main interest was in examining the effects of valence and arousal on participants' target detection times, we created scores for each emotional target category that controlled for the participant's RTs to detect neutral targets (e.g., subtracting the RT to detect neutral targets from the RT to detect positive high arousal targets). These difference scores were then examined with a 2 × 2 × 2 (Age [young, older] × Valence [positive, negative] × Arousal [high, low]) analysis of variance (ANOVA). This ANOVA revealed only a significant main effect of arousal, $F(1, 46) = 8.41$, $p = .006$, $\eta_p^2 = .16$, with larger differences between neutral and high arousal images ($M = 137$) than between neutral and low arousal images ($M = 93$; i.e., high arousal items processed more quickly across both age groups compared with low arousal items; see Figure 1). There was no significant main effect for valence, nor was there an interaction between valence and arousal. It is critical that the analysis revealed only a main effect of age but no interactions with age. Thus, the arousal-mediated effects on detection time appeared stable in young and older adults.

APA CODES: 4.22–4.30

Review Exercises: Abbreviations

Analyses focus on participants' reaction times (RTs) to the 120 trials in which a target was present and was from a different emotional category from the distractor (for example, RTs were not included for arrays containing eight images of a cat and one image of a butterfly because cats and butterflies are both positive low arousal items). Reaction times were analyzed for 24 trials of each target emotion category. Reaction times for error trials were excluded (fewer than 5% of all responses) as were reaction times that were ±3 standard deviations from each participant's M (approximately 1.5% of responses). Median RTs were then calculated for each of the five emotional target categories, collapsing across array type (see Table 2 for raw RT values for each of the two age groups). This allowed us to examine, e.g., whether participants were faster to detect images of snakes than images of mushrooms, regardless of the type of array in which they were presented. Because our main interest was in examining the effects of valence and arousal on participants' target detection times, we created scores for each emotional target category that controlled for the participant's reaction times to detect neutral targets (e.g., subtracting the RT to detect neutral targets from the RT to detect positive high arousal targets). These difference scores were then examined with a $2 \times 2 \times 2$ (Age [young, older] $\times$ Valence [positive, negative] $\times$ Arousal [high, low]) ANOVA. This ANOVA revealed only a significant main effect of arousal, $F(1, 46) = 8.41$, $p = .006$, $\eta_p^2 = .16$, with larger differences between neutral and high arousal images ($M = 137$) than between neutral and low arousal images ($M = 93$; that is, high arousal items processed more quickly across both age groups compared with low arousal items; see Figure 1). There was no significant main effect for valence, nor was there an interaction between valence and arousal. It is critical that the analysis revealed only a main effect of age but no interactions with age. Thus, the arousal-mediated effects on detection time appeared stable in young and older adults.

APA CODES: 4.22–4.30

Review Exercise: Numbers

The 60 studies published between 1969 and 1988 that reported evaluations of treatments for extreme fear reactions to a specific fictional character from a book, TV, or film (*monstrophobia*) were reviewed, and a meta-analysis of the results was performed.

The participants in the different studies were male and female individuals ranging in age from 3 to 96 years old who had reported a phobic reaction to at least one character. As assessed by self-report (in 40 of the studies), the mean duration of exposure to the character prior to development of the phobic reaction was 4 min. The participants in 37 of the studies reported a phobic reaction to only one character; the participants in 12 of the studies reported a phobic reaction to two characters; the participants in seven of the studies reported a phobic reaction to one or two characters; and the participants in the remaining four studies reported a reaction to as few as one character and as many as seven different characters. There were nine different characters reported as phobic objects by one or more clients in the different studies: the Wicked Witch of the East, the Wicked Witch of the West, the Phantom of the Opera, Dr. Frankenstein, Dr. Frankenstein's Monster, Medusa, the Big Bad Wolf, Jaws, and Cookie Monster. Twenty-eight of the studies (including 823 participants) reported data on the number of additional phobias (other than monstrophobia) reported by the participants; on the basis of those data, the mean number of additional phobias was 0.16.

Studies were included in the evaluation if they compared a treatment with a no-treatment control or with at least one other treatment. In actuality the different studies assessed 1, 2, 3, or 6 different treatment methods. Treatments lasted from 1 day to 8 months and from 1 to 50 sessions. Participants were treated individually or in groups of up to eight participants per group. The sample sizes for a given treatment ranged from 1 to 24 in the individual studies. Combining all of the studies, the number of participants who received each treatment ranged from 14 to 238, and the total number of participants was 1,942.

The 60 studies are listed in Table 1, with an indication of which of eight different treatments (two behavioral methods [desensitization and flooding], cognitive therapy, rational therapy, client-centered therapy, psychodynamic therapy, hypnosis, and a form of eclectic talk therapy) were assessed in the study, the sample size for each treatment, and the duration of each treatment. Overall, the correlation between number of phobic characters and treatment effectiveness was −.38, and the correlation between number of sessions and treatment effectiveness was .46.

APA CODES: 4.31–4.38

Review Exercise: Numbers

The sixty studies published between 1969 and 1988 that reported evaluations of treatments for extreme fear reactions to a specific fictional character from a book, TV, or film (*monstrophobia*) were reviewed, and a meta-analysis of the results was performed.

The participants in the different studies were male and female individuals ranging in age from three to 96 years old who had reported a phobic reaction to at least 1 character. As assessed by self-report (in 40 of the studies), the mean duration of exposure to the character prior to development of the phobic reaction was 4 min. The participants in 37 of the studies reported a phobic reaction to only 1 character; the participants in 12 of the studies reported a phobic reaction to two characters; the participants in 7 of the studies reported a phobic reaction to one or two characters; and the participants in the remaining 4 studies reported a reaction to as few as one character and as many as seven different characters. There were nine different characters reported as phobic objects by 1 or more clients in the different studies: the Wicked Witch of the East, the Wicked Witch of the West, the Phantom of the Opera, Dr. Frankenstein, Dr. Frankenstein's Monster, Medusa, the Big Bad Wolf, Jaws, and Cookie Monster. 28 of the studies (including 823 participants) reported data on the number of additional phobias (other than monstrophobia) reported by the participants; on the basis of those data, the mean number of additional phobias was .16.

Studies were included in the evaluation if they compared a treatment with a no-treatment control or with at least one other treatment. In actuality, the different studies assessed one, two, three, or six different treatment methods. Treatments lasted from one day to eight months and from 1 to 50 sessions. Participants were treated individually or in groups of up to 8 participants per group. The sample sizes for a given treatment ranged from 1 to 24 in the individual studies. Combining all of the studies, the number of participants who received each treatment ranged from 14 to 238, and the total number of participants was 1942.

The 60 studies are listed in Table I, with an indication of which of 8 different treatments (2 behavioral methods [desensitization and flooding], cognitive therapy, rational therapy, client-centered therapy, psychodynamic therapy, hypnosis, and a form of eclectic talk therapy) were assessed in the study, the sample size for each treatment, and the duration of each treatment. Overall, the correlation between number of phobic characters and treatment effectiveness was −0.38, and the correlation between number of sessions and treatment effectiveness was +0.46.

APA CODES: 4.31–4.38

Review Exercise: Metrication

To determine two-point thresholds, point distance and point pressure were varied. Point distance was measured in millimeters, and pressure was measured in grams. The lower lips of subjects were taped to a 2-cm × 3-cm plastic restrainer. Some male orangutans required slightly larger restrainers. Pictures and words were then presented to the orangutans with the lowest thresholds. Pictures were 3 ft (0.91 m) high and 4 ft (1.21 m) long. Words were 2 m high and 4 m long. Identification reaction time was recorded in milliseconds.

APA CODES: 4.39–4.40

Review Exercise: Metrication

To determine two-point thresholds, point distance and point pressure were varied. Point distance was measured in mms, and pressure was measured in grams. The lower lips of subjects were taped to a 2- × 3-centimeter plastic restrainer. Some male orangutans required slightly larger restrainers. Pictures and words were then presented to the orangutans with the lowest thresholds. Pictures were 3 feet high and 4 feet long. Words were 2 m high and 4 m long. Identification reaction time was recorded in milliseconds.

APA CODES: 4.39–4.40

Review Exercise: Statistical and Mathematical Copy

Results and Discussion

Figure 5 shows the mean phoneme boundaries for all conditions and the restoration effect for the captor condition. There was a highly significant effect of condition on the phoneme boundary values, $F(4, 44) = 26.87$, $p < .001$. Incrementing the level of the fourth harmonic lowered the phoneme boundary relative to the vowel-alone condition (by 48 Hz, $p < .001$), indicating that the extra energy was integrated into the vowel percept. The lagging-fourth condition had a significantly higher phoneme boundary than the incremented-fourth condition ($p < .001$), but the boundary did not return all the way to that for the vowel-alone condition ($p < .005$). Compared with the effect of a lead time of the same duration (240 ms), the offset asynchrony was only about half as effective. The size of the boundary return (22 Hz) is broadly comparable to that obtained for similar stimuli by Darwin and Sutherland (1984). The mean restoration effect was very small and did not differ significantly from 0, $t(11) = 0.29$, $p = .775$. The captor-control condition was not significantly different from the incremented-fourth condition. These results indicate that the captor has little or no effect in this context. In terms of an inhibition-based account, this finding is consistent with an effect of neural rebound at captor offset but not with sustained inhibition when the captor is present. Note that the formation of a perceptual group comprising the captor and the lagging portion of the added 500-Hz tone should lead to a significant restoration effect.

APA CODES: 4.44–4.46

Review Exercise: Statistical and Mathematical Copy

Results and Discussion

Figure 5 shows the mean phoneme boundaries for all conditions and the restoration effect for the captor condition. There was a highly significant effect of condition on the phoneme boundary values, F (df = 4/44) = 26.87, p<.001. Incrementing the level of the fourth harmonic lowered the phoneme boundary relative to the vowel-alone condition (by 48 Hz, p<.001), indicating that the extra energy was integrated into the vowel percept. The lagging-fourth condition had a significantly higher phoneme boundary than the incremented-fourth condition (p<.001), but the boundary did not return all the way to that for the vowel-alone condition (p<.005). Compared with the effect of a lead time of the same duration (240 ms), the offset asynchrony was only about half as effective. The size of the boundary return (22 Hz) is broadly comparable to that obtained for similar stimuli by Darwin and Sutherland (1984). The mean restoration effect was very small and did not differ significantly from 0, t (df = 11) = 0.29, p=.775. The captor-control condition was not significantly different from the incremented-fourth condition. These results indicate that the captor has little or no effect in this context. In terms of an inhibition-based account, this finding is consistent with an effect of neural rebound at captor offset but not with sustained inhibition when the captor is present. Note that the formation of a perceptual group comprising the captor and the lagging portion of the added 500-Hz tone should lead to a significant restoration effect.

APA CODES: 4.44–4.46

Review Exercise: Tables

Table 5

Hierarchical Multiple Regression Analyses Predicting Postabortion Positive Well-Being From Preabortion Social Support and Preabortion Social Conflict With Mother, Partner, and Friend

| | Source of social support and social conflict | | | | | |
| | Mother | | Partner | | Friend | |
Predictor	ΔR^2	β	ΔR^2	β	ΔR^2	β
Step 1	.13*		.10***		.10***	
Control variables[a]						
Step 2	.16***		.19***		.22***	
Positive affect		.31***		.32***		.35***
Negative affect		−.25***		−.27***		−.30***
Step 3	.02		.05***		.01*	
Social support		.17*		.17***		.08†
Social conflict		.09		−.08		−.06
Step 4	.01		.00		.00	
Social Support × Social Conflict		−.14		−.00		−.07
Total R^2	.32***		.33***		.34***	
N	153		455		373	

Note. Adapted from "Mixed Messages: Implications of Social Conflict and Social Support Within Close Relationships for Adjustment to a Stressful Life Event," by B. Major, J. M. Zubek, M. L. Cooper, C. Cozzarelli, and C. Richards, 1997, *Journal of Personality and Social Psychology, 72,* p. 1359. Copyright 1997 by the American Psychological Association.

[a]Control variables included age, race, education, marital status, religion, abortion history, depression history, and prior mental health counseling.

†$p < .10$. *$p < .05$. ***$p < .001$.

APA CODES: 5.07–5.19

Review Exercise: Tables

Table 5

Hierarchical multiple regression analyses predicting postabortion positive well-being from preabortion social support and preabortion social conflict with mother, partner, and friend

| | Source of Social Support and Social Conflict | | | | | |
| | Mother | | Partner | | Friend | |
Predictor	ΔR^2	β	ΔR^2	β	ΔR^2	β
Step 1	.13*		.10***		.10***	
Control Variables[a]						
Step 2	.16***		.19***		.22***	
Positive Affect		.31***		.32***		.35***
Negative Affect		−.25***		−.27***		−.30***
Step 3	.02		.05***		.01*	
Social Support		.17*		.17***		.08†
Social Conflict		.09		−.08		−.06
Step 4	.01		.00		.00	
Social Support × Social Conflict		−.14		−.00		−.07
Total R^2	.32***		.33***		.34***	
n	153		455		373	

Note. Adapted from "Mixed Messages: Implications of Social Conflict and Social Support Within Close Relationships for Adjustment to a Stressful Life Event," by B. Major, J. M. Zubek, M. L. Cooper, C. Cozzarelli, and C. Richards, 1997, *Journal of Personality and Social Psychology, 72,* p. 1359. Copyright 1997 by the American Psychological Association.

[a]Control variables included age, race, education, marital status, religion, abortion history, depression history, and prior mental health counseling.

†$p < .10$. *$p < .05$. ***$p < .001$.

APA CODES: 5.07–5.19

Research Report Mastery Tests

The *Instructor's Resource Guide* contains four mastery tests for each unit (term paper and research report). Your instructor will decide whether to give you one or more mastery tests as a means of evaluating your knowledge of APA Style and your readiness to prepare writing assignments. These tests are similar in structure and content to the familiarization and practice tests but contain different questions. Your instructor will provide you with the mastery tests and may or may not grade them; a grade is useful only for demonstrating that you have mastered APA Style (90% correct is the standard for mastery unless your instructor announces otherwise).

Like the familiarization and practice tests, the mastery tests contain approximately 40 multiple-choice questions, along with the APA codes indicating where in the *Publication Manual* you can find the answers. However, you may not use the *Publication Manual* as you take the tests. Your instructor will give you a grade and feedback about any areas in which you need further work.